DETROIT'S
DELECTABLE
PAST

DETROIT'S
DELECTABLE
PAST

Two Centuries of Frog Legs, Pigeon Pie & Drugstore Whiskey

BILL LOOMIS

THE
History
PRESS

Published by The History Press
Charleston, SC 29403
www.historypress.net

Front cover images, top left: Pioneers along the Detroit–Chicago Road, by Roy C. Gamble, depicting pioneers on the Detroit–Chicago Road, which is now Michigan Avenue. They are guided by Lewis Cass (in the top hat) and Father Gabriel Richard (wearing a priest's hat and cloak). Both men were instrumental in getting the road built. *Collections of the Michigan Historical Museum, www. michigan.gov/museum. Top right:* Jessie DeBoth with cooking students. *U.S. Library of Congress.*

First published 2012

ISBN 978.1.5402.3179.6

Library of Congress CIP data applied for.

Contents

CONTENTS

Acknowledgements

Many thanks to Joe Gartrell, who persisted in seeing this through.

Pam Shermeyer, the online editor of the *Detroit News*, published several of these articles, sometimes in slightly different formats, including "Living It Up in Old Detroit: Restaurants, Taverns and Low-Lit Saloons," "Christmas in Old Detroit," "To Market, To Market," "The Milk Peddlers' War," "Fishing for a Living in Detroit" and "Passenger Pigeons' Last Stand." Pam's help with editing my sprawling articles has been invaluable.

Mr. Ralph Naveaux, historian and an expert on the French history of Monroe and Detroit, was kind enough to review some of the French history of several articles, especially "Wild Game on the Table."

The Hoyt Library, an excellent archive of the Saginaw Public Library, provided assistance on W.B. Mershon and the plight of the passenger pigeons.

Thanks also to:

The Dearborn Archive's Ken Erwood, for his very helpful research.

The Farmington Public Library, Heritage Collection.

David Berg and the Michigan State University libraries, for permission to use images from the "Feeding America" archive of American cookbooks.

John Einhaus, who was a great help with technical issues on illustrations.

Barney Klein, for his brilliant photographic skills.

And my Hogshead Buddies, for their encouragement and cheerful bonhomie.

Most importantly, this book is dedicated to my children—Evan, Claire, Sydney and Natasha—and to my wife, Janice, for her support, great sacrifice and levelheaded advice. All my love.

Introduction

Tell me what you eat, and I shall tell you what you are.
—Jean Anthelme Brillat-Savarin

That often-quoted aphorism was written to a friend and published in 1825. While Brillat-Savarin (who once dined with George Washington in New York City) intended his wise rule to apply to individuals, it could well work for entire cities. Like Detroit. And for this book, his aphorism is tweaked once more: "Tell me what you *ate*, and I'll tell you what you *were*." This is because this is the history of eating food in Detroit. But it is more than eating food. It is culinary history—the point, purpose and fun of everything involving food, drink and dining.

For instance, if you said you ate whatever you could shoot, served it with flour gravy and washed it all down with crust coffee, you might have been a settler in Farmington in 1835. If you sat down to twelve-course dinners with toe-tapping band music, you were likely a Victorian industrialist or lumber baron. If you ate mooshrats (muskrats), frog legs and lots of duck, you likely came from Monroe.

Food history is all-encompassing, from growing and hunting to processing and preparing, from shopping and cooking to eating and overeating and from dining and drinking to cleaning up—then doing it all over again. This was everyday life in Detroit from the earliest French era to the start of the twentieth century.

The Crystal Ballroom of the Statler Hotel in Detroit. *Author's collection.*

Some dishes and recipes are everlasting, like expertly grilled steaks on a hearth in 1817. The only thing to change in the Thanksgiving feast since its inception has been the size of the turkey; your great-great-grandmother might feel right at home at your Thanksgiving table. On the other hand, some cherished dishes are forgotten. Detroiters served their guests Charlotte Russe, a dessert, for over 150 years, but today few people have heard of it. Tongue sandwiches were eaten at children's parties of the wealthy, something that is not going to happen these days. Detroit restaurants were once famous across the United States for one thing: frog legs. And the most popular roast for Sunday dinner, mutton, is very hard to find today.

Important events occurred due to food and drink. Michigan was the first in the United States to mandate that all milk be pasteurized due to the relentless fight of Detroit's health officer, Dr. William Price. One sees how profound an effect the opening of the Erie Canal had on Detroit's pantries and dining tables.

For some, food was a livelihood: commercial fishing on the Detroit River, running a tavern, selling vegetables at the farmers' markets, peddling milk or driving livestock on the hoof up Grand River Avenue. It could be argued that food was even more important one to two hundred years ago; in the past, medicine might be whiskey and doctors were few, so Detroit women nursed children, healed injured husbands and relieved aging parents with their cooking—and other *peculiar* concoctions ("toad ointment for caked breasts" leaps to mind). Cookbooks for invalids, such as Dr. A.W. Chase's from Ann Arbor, had over eight hundred recipes and were bestsellers in the 1860s. Chase sold four million copies.

This book does not cover food and Detroit chronologically; it does not read like a history book. Chapters cover subjects, such as how Detroit celebrated Christmases past, what hotel dinners were like in 1840 and taking cooking classes in 1890.

The Importance of Grilled Lamb Chops

The greatest impression one gets reading everyday voices from the past is how immediately one feels connected to these people. A little girl with her family heading to the great American West to find their new home tastes her first grilled lamb chop. It was cooked up by Sally Ten Eyck at the Ten Eyck Tavern in Dearborn in 1830, and it still sounds absolutely delicious.

Another impression is how unique Detroit once was and still is. For many years before the Civil War, tourists came to Detroit to experience a city where inhabitants had already lived for two hundred years yet seemed to be on the outpost of the civilized world. After the American Revolution, while technically an American city, French Detroiters and the native Indian tribes were not Americans. They were culturally different, and their legacy continues with us.

Many people today believe that two hundred years ago most people ate only salt pork and biscuits. Some did, but reading through a Detroit cookbook of the past shows the immense variety of food women cooked even before cooking stoves were brought into homes. Today, it is not unusual to find children and even adults who, in their entire lives, have eaten mostly cold cereal, pizza and chicken nuggets. The variety of food our ancestors ate is striking. When one reads about past Detroiters' cooking, parties, cooking classes, infant feedings, Christmas dinners, gentlemen's late-night suppers, weddings, what they ordered at lunch during work, what they bought at the farmers' market or what they fed invalids, one is amazed, even bewildered, but also comforted. But that's what food does.

PART I
ON THE TOWN

1

Living It Up in Old Detroit

Restaurants, Taverns and Low-Lit Saloons

Before the famous Delmonico's restaurant opened in New York City in 1845, there were no restaurants in the United States as we know them today. There were, however, "eating houses." Detroit had its share, usually attached to saloons. Food was served, often to encourage more drinking. The following advertisement proclaimed a new enterprise in 1850:

> *Patrick Collins has opened a new Eating House on Griswold Street. Mr. Collins is a stirring man and of course will be successful. The arrangements are all "tip-top."*

Eating houses featured specialties like all-you-can-eat oysters or green turtle soup; they usually announced "a good accommodation for victuals" such as soup, potatoes, beef, ham and so forth. Nevertheless, complaints about the food were common. With the arrival of the famous French chef and cooking instructor Professor Pierre Blot in New York City in 1865, the Detroit editorials hoped that students of Mr. Blot could "relieve the country from the reproach of having but one gravy."

The Steamboat Hotel was one of the oldest and most popular hotels in Detroit during the early nineteenth century. It was owned by Ben Woodruff. *Illustration courtesy of Silas Farmer.*

Restaurant Riots

The earliest restaurants appeared in the 1870s in Detroit, and by 1899, Detroit had 169. People had come to rely on restaurants for lunch and dinner, and night-shift workers, many living in lodging houses with no kitchens, began to depend on restaurants throughout the night as their only source of cooked meals. (Prior to the 1870s, most single men lived in boardinghouses. A boardinghouse provided room and food. Later, as salaries in Detroit and the United States overall tightened, single men were usually found in less respectable "lodging houses," which were simply rooms.)

In 1918, a series of riots broke out in Detroit when William K. Prudden, the state coal director for Michigan, ordered restaurants and all "nonessential businesses" closed in a plan to save coal fuel during a winter shortage. Thousands of hungry and angry night workers hit the streets, and the order was immediately rescinded.

RESTAURANTS AND SOCIAL CLASS

Detroit restaurants were in many cases categorized by the social class of their customers. Aside from in the first-class restaurants, there was no menu to choose from; you got what was served that day. On the low end was "a meal for a nickel." Nickel meals were served down by the docks in the bars where the ruffians and machine shop laborers might show up. For a nickel, you got a bowl of soup and bread or pork and beans.

Dinner for a dime was advertised in front of restaurants, which many times displayed their offerings that day with sample platters set on a chair or table inside the door. This might include a long-braised cut of beef, sauerkraut and a piece of buttered johnny bread (corn bread). Next to this array was typically a platter of buttered potatoes. Other days, the offerings might be potpie, corned beef and cabbage or pork roast. Your beverage choices were coffee, tea or milk (soda pop did not yet exist). Dessert was pudding.

People ate at the bar or at small wooden tables; the food was brought by waitresses, who in 1899 were called "restaurant girls." A bit later, they were called "waiting girls," which then turned into waitresses. They worked for salary, with no tips. In better establishments, tipping was considered insulting. The waitress uniform began in 1915 in New York City and spread across the country. It started as a plain black dress, white apron and white cap.

A restaurant girl was interviewed in Philadelphia and asked how she liked the occupation in 1896:

> *Q: What do you think of restaurant work?*
> *A: Think of it?* [Laughs] *Oh, all we restaurant girls think there is nothing like it…Of course the work is hard. You don't get many chances to sit down…The life is a bright one…The life of restaurant girls has a change of faces. We see new faces and get new ideas for dresses and bonnets from the women patrons. Of course, the work never changes a jot but the changing faces keeps us from getting in a rut and keeps us younger and gayer in feelings.*

Moving up the restaurant scale, a meal for fifteen to twenty cents got you more choices. This meal offered two meats such as corned beef and cabbage or a Detroit favorite, "city chicken," which was actually cubed pork or veal shoulder skewered on sticks (something to vaguely resemble chicken drumsticks) and braised in sauce. Veal and pork were cheaper than chicken in those days. In addition, you could take tomato soup, beets, pickles and bread and butter. Along with pudding, apple pie was offered.

These restaurants advertised that they used the "card system": "One can pick out just as much or as little as one wants." Stepping it up further, for twenty-five cents you had a substantial choice. The following was the bill of fare for a quarter:

> *Broiled trout with egg sauce*
> *Roast short ribs of beef. Brown potatoes. Broiled English mutton chops.*
> *Baked potatoes.*
> *Stewed Spring Lamb Petit pois.*
> *These are served with desserts, coffee, tea, cider, beer or ale.*

For fifty cents, you could dine in the finest restaurants in Detroit, perhaps at the Hotel Cadillac Café, the toast of Detroit in 1892. It was very progressive, serving both accompanied and unaccompanied women. You were attended by a waiter wearing a formal dress coat. Dress coats were at times the source of labor disputes between waiters and restaurant management, as the uniform was expensive to maintain in the mandated spotless condition—especially during the winter "off season," after the holidays, when dining traffic slowed and management would cut salaries.

The dinner menu would take a normal patron two hours to get through. It typically began with consommé, followed by fish, beef, turkey, duck, wild game and shrimp, all with sherbet served between meals. And of course, patrons had many choices of desserts. In these high-end restaurants, little was subtle or restrained; the dining room appeared plated with gold, bejeweled with crystal or swathed in purple velvet. The Hotel Cadillac Café centerpiece for a reception in 1904 held for Miss Valerie Etheridge Moran and E. Leydon Ford was an example, as reported in the *Detroit Free Press*:

> *The table, twenty eight feet long and six feet wide, was set in the center with a mammoth electrical fountain spraying water from four founts; the basin was ten feet long and three feet wide and was inlaid with red, white and blue electric lights and sprayed water also from its four sides into the*

center. The lights caught the water and flashed it in many delicate hues, while goldfish in keeping with the colors glided here and there among the varicolored lights in the basin. Around the edges were seashore stones and otherwise the table was a solid mass of costly flowers.

ETHNIC RESTAURANTS

As early as the 1860s, advertisements appeared for Italian, French, Greek, Venetian, German and Polish restaurants. However, the most popular were Chinese restaurants. The first Detroit Chinese restaurant seemed to serve only two dishes: bird's nest soup and chop suey. A restaurant review described the exotic décor at the Oriental Café:

The ceilings are painted to represent the blue sky...Looking up one sees the blue sky and the clouds. In the night the light is furnished from above, but to carry out the illusion the moon and stars shine out in splendor and some of the electric lights are held in place by birds.

Detroit boasted twelve Chinese restaurants in the early twentieth century. Dining at them was an escape from mundane life, with all the ethnic clichés firmly exploited. One restaurant on Larned Street was busted in 1906 for housing an opium den in the basement, where the newspapers reported white women "hit the pipe" in "dark, smutty rooms." Racist stereotypes notwithstanding, the food remained popular with Detroiters. A 1912 Oriental Café bill of fare advertised for $1.75 included:

Mandarin Cocktail
Soup
Bird's nest Sub Gum

Relishes
Chinese Chow Chow
Fish
Fish Rolled with Walnuts
Entrees
Spring Wings Peking Style

Sauté of Duck's Liver with Pickled Egg Noble Fashion
Roast
Emperor Pan Roast Jumbo Squab
Salad Vegetables
Coffee Tea

TAVERNS AND INNS

Although the term "tavern" was used loosely, it typically meant a restaurant/bar with rooms for overnight travelers located on the major roads outside the city. There was Ruff's Place, Buckin's Tavern, Sheldon's Tavern and Marsten's, to name a few. They served travelers, drovers and their crews, teamsters, local farmers, sometimes soldiers and families migrating to the American West.

A longtime favorite on Grand River Avenue was the Weston Inn, better known later as the Botsford Inn. In 1836, Orrin and Allen Weston built a large family home/inn named the Weston House alongside what would become the Grand River Turnpike. Another of the most beloved by pioneering families was the Old Ten Eyck Tavern in Dearborn, founded in 1826. It was located on the Chicago Road (Michigan Avenue) nine miles from the city.

Running a tavern involved long hours of hard work. The Wayside Inn, located closer to Detroit, served primarily hog, sheep and cattle drovers. A drover was a team of men and their shepherd dogs paid to move forty or fifty animals on the hoof down the big roads to the city markets or slaughterhouses. In the evening, the drovers would arrive at a tavern, where their livestock had to be penned, watered and fed while the drover team ate dinner and went to bed. Teams kept arriving until eleven or twelve o'clock at night.

This was a rough clientele. The following *Detroit Free Press* interview was with a retired tavern keep who owned a tavern in the 1840s:

> *In the house it was worse than in the barns. The drovers and their boys would be awful hungry, and the way they would hide victuals was a whole show. The tables were occupied from early morning to late at night...All my girls could do was bring more, more all the time...And it was just as*

On the Town

In 1836, Orrin and Allen Weston built a large family home/inn named the Weston House alongside what would become the Grand River Turnpike. In the mid-1800s, it was bought by Milton Botsford. *Farmington Public Library Heritage Collection.*

bad with the cooks. The stoves were hot all the time…By 3 o'clock [in the morning] *those drovers who got in early the night before and were abed by 9 o'clock, would be up, stamping around the house, shouting for their breakfast and pounding on the bar for me to come down and give them their bitters. I couldn't stand it now.*

The taverns disappeared with the arrival of train travel.

ROADHOUSES AND SALOONS

Roadhouses were located on the outskirts of Detroit in Highland Park, Hamtramck, Royal Oak or Pontiac with such names as La Belle Inn off Woodward, Marquette's and Crooked Acres at Seven Mile Road and

The Griswold Bar was in the Hotel Griswold at Griswold and Grand River. This photo was taken sometime between 1905 and 1920. *U.S. Library of Congress.*

Woodward. They were outside the city to keep out of the eye of the police, since they were often the source of crime and trouble up through the 1920s. Anyone could drink at a roadhouse, and these establishments frequently served hard liquor to boys as young as twelve. Some had illegal slot machines, hosted "cocking mains" (cock fights) and frightened local farm families with brawls, robbery and gunfights. They flouted the no-alcohol-on-Sundays law and were called by one Hamtramck sheriff "a menace to the peaceable citizens of the village."

In the city, Detroit had between 500 and 600 saloons in the 1850s to 1860s. By 1915, that number had risen to 1,700. The proportion was described as one saloon to every fifty families. While the wealthy had their clubs and the hotels, the workingman had his saloons (women were not permitted in saloons).

Saloons were also a reflection of contemporary society in Detroit and throughout the United States. From the 1850s to the turn of the century,

On the Town

a significant percentage of American cities were made up of bachelor men as part of the industrialization and geographic expansion westward. Some of the young men came from Detroit families, while others arrived from all parts of the country and overseas. In an excellent book by John Schneider, *Detroit and the Problem of Order, 1830–1880: A Geography of Crime, Riot and Policing*, on policing and keeping order in Detroit during this era, Schneider refers to this issue as forming a "bachelor transient sub-culture." Their numbers surged at the end of the Civil War, and the bachelors and their bachelor activities began to frighten the established society, whose businesses and homes were adjacent to those areas where young men hung out and looked for ways to entertain themselves. Saloons were one activity; billiards, introduced in the 1850s, was another; and brothels were a third source of entertainment.

The *Detroit Daily* of 1871 described a saloon as a hangout:

> *Young men comes in and sets around the table talking for an hour yet, and drink only one glass apiece. They don't seem to want much beer, but they got not other place to go.*

The saloons and brothels that catered to this group were mostly located along the Detroit River, with a great many in a dangerous slum east of Woodward called "the Potomac." Just north of Jefferson was another smaller hangout called "the Heights." These areas were adjacent to wealthy homes and split "Piety Hill," the wealthy church-lined street east of Jefferson Avenue. During the decades following the Civil War, the public's attitude toward these men shifted; as much as they were admired during the Civil War, years after the war they were feared and referred to as "floaters" or "rootless drifters" who were simply lazy and refused to look for work. After the Civil War, some men who returned to the city were thought to have psychological disturbances and violent outbursts from their traumatic experiences on Civil War battlefields. There was no police protection until 1868, when the city formed a police department. Before then, Detroiters were protected by ineffectual sheriffs and "ward constables." Private armed guards were hired for retail shops and businesses. During the 1860s, fear of mugging, burglary and rape was constant, and the saloons were viewed as the source of this activity.

A large portion of the saloons were owned by brewers, such as Stroh Brewing. The big breweries would fund a new owner by paying for the saloon, furnishing it and stocking it with liquor. In return, the new owner

Billy Boushaw was a colorful figure in old Detroit. He was the owner of flophouses and the infamous Bucket of Blood Tavern. *Author's collection.*

was expected to sell only the brewer's brand of beer. But the new owners seldom stayed true, and when a cheaper beer was offered, they switched.

Saloons were the source of endless maudlin dramas of drunken husbands, deserted wives and broken families. In one court proceeding, the wife declared, "He was a shiftless man who didn't care what happened as long as he could have his cigars and sit in saloons and play cards."

Saloons were frequently political hangouts, as well. The Detroit bar Sharp's was known as "a sporting and political headquarters." From 1908 to 1917, Billy Boushaw owned a notorious saloon in the first precinct of the first ward. Boushaw called himself "king of the precinct" and "foist of the foist." His saloon, the Bucket of Blood Tavern, and boardinghouse (actually a flophouse for sailors) were at 111 and 115 Atwater Street, respectively. He lived above the saloon. Boushaw helped down-and-out "floaters" and dockworkers in the infamous river precinct and, in return, got their votes. Boushaw controlled the 1914 Detroit city election. A 1908 newspaper editorial voiced its opinion of Boushaw:

> *Probably the most startling thing that would catch the eye of the most casual observer is the condition of affairs in the first precinct of the first ward, where ex-convicts, thugs, thieves, and booze grafters swarm the*

election booth and rule the day...It is notable that no less than 27 votes were enrolled from Billy Boushaw's tough lodging house and saloon...for the most part it is a tough set that frequent the place—scum.

THE RAJAH OF SWILL POINT

In the mid-nineteenth century, there was a whiskey distillery at the corner of First and Jefferson Streets that, along with producing barrels of whiskey, discharged mountains of swill, the grain slurry from making whiskey. Dairy farmers from around the city would line up their wagons to load swill for their cows and livestock. The distillery closed and went elsewhere, but the blocks surrounding it became known as "Swill Point." By the 1870s and 1880s, this area was one of four notorious slums in Detroit. Police were afraid to go into Swill Point, the Potomac, Kentucky or the Heights. The streets of Swill Point were described in the newspapers as "badly illuminated at night by the lights of dozens of low saloons." The saloons had colorful names like the Slaughter Pen or House of Lords. They were owned by characters such as the notorious Dan Hanrahan or Jem Cummerford, called the Rajah of Swill Point, who always carried a revolver and tended to use it when drunk, which was constantly.

A JOLLY WINTER TOUR OF THE SLUMS

In the 1880s, as the police began to gain some control over crime and rioting, it became a fad in big American cities for young people of wealthy families to tour slums, jails, ethnic neighborhoods and generally dangerous places. Like New Yorkers and Bostonians, in Detroit small groups of couples from areas of the city such as Piety Hill would gather on Saturday nights in winter, hitch up sleighs and head down to Swill Point under a police escort. These were young married couples who, according to a newspaper of the day, had "never been more than a stone's throw from the major thoroughfares or promenades of the city." They rode in a roomy sleigh pulled by four horses.

A Woodward snowy evening, circa 1899. *U.S. Library of Congress.*

The tour started at the Brush Street Electric Works, where the superintendent of the facility gave them a tour and demonstrated how electric light bulbs were made. Then they entered Swill Point and looked into a saloon, where a prostitute named Maud Doyle had not long ago committed suicide by poison in Jem Cummerford's "grog shop." Then they inspected the "bummer's rest," or Woodbridge Street Police station, where Sergeant Noble led them to meet fifteen prisoners. One female prisoner fell to her knees screaming and pleading for help to be let out, with zero effect. The eager group was then led to the basement to visit the tramps' lodging, but they did not stay long due to the suffocating furnace heat and nauseating stench. They continued their night at another station in the Potomac and Heights slums, where the women were encouraged to sit in a paddy wagon and toured more cells. Then the police escort called in the guitar and harmonica orchestra for an impromptu concert.

The "slummers" ended up in the German gathering spot Arbeiter Halle. This was the famous gathering hall for Germans in Detroit and throughout

Arbeiter Halle (Workers Hall) in 1903. Arbeiter Halle was the center of German social and political life in Detroit and Michigan until the 1930s, when it was demolished.

the state of Michigan for many decades. The hall could get a bit combative politically, with union, socialist, communist and even anarchist meetings, but this night there was a party of three hundred dancers whooping it up, with a big band playing German dance hall favorites. By now it was one o'clock in the morning, and the group was famished. They had pretzels and fragrant Schweitzer sandwiches (which were not popular due to the stinky German cheese); however, the novel hot Frankfurter sausages hit the spot, and they danced for hours, ending up at home at three o'clock in the morning.

2

Dinner Parties during Detroit's Gilded Age

T he Gilded Age is usually associated with New York or Philadelphia, but it was very much a part of life in Detroit. Detroiters had been making money since the 1850s, and what they now sought was class—and fun. Detroit wives living on West Lafayette Street entertained "at home" on Tuesday, with flowers, food and music in the drawing room waiting for friends and callers. People had ninety-foot yachts that they moored at the Detroit Yacht Club. Daughters of Michigan lumber barons, steel makers or railroad tycoons married European aristocracy.

In 1835, the population of Detroit was about 3,000. By the Civil War, thirty years later, the population had grown to over 45,000, and by the 1890s, it was over 130,000. Everyone belonged to a club of some sort. There were dozens of gentlemen's clubs, lodges and secret societies, such as the Order of Chosen Friends, the Benevolent and Protective Order of Beavers (for saloonkeepers), the United Ancient Order of Druids and the Detroit Federation of Homing Pigeon Fanciers. The more well-known clubs, such as the Shriners and Elks, had thousands of members, and people looked forward all year to their dinners, parties and dances. The headline from a Detroit newspaper captures that spirit:

> *Women of Elks Parties Are Most Enthusiastic in Keeping Up with Husbands in Pleasures of Entertainment. Members of the Grand Lodge and their ladies were given a generous sample of why life is worth living in Detroit.*

The Detroit Club is at 712 Cass Avenue. The building was constructed in 1891 and listed on the National Register of Historic Places in 2005. This picture dates from 1899.

The classiest of the men's clubs in 1893 was the Detroit Club, located at the corner of Cass and Fort Streets. Here mingled bank presidents, mine owners, editors, manufacturers, railroad presidents, architects, professors and more. A description of the club from an article in the *Detroit Free Press* in 1893 gives an idea of its luxury:

> *There is a reception room unsurpassed in the west, a library of valuable books and a wealth of interesting current literature, a large fully equipped dining room, several smaller dining rooms for private use, a café, a billiard and pool room, bowling alley, card rooms, barber shop, complete toilet facilities in every part of the building. The reception room for the gentler sex is a bower of beauty…The dinners and suppers held within its walls are marvels of completeness and elegance.*

On the Town

THE FRENCH DETROIT DINNER PARTY

Of course, dinner parties did not start in the Victorian days. Detroiters had been throwing parties for 150 years before that. French Detroit weddings were lavish without the formal stiffness of later affairs. They were actually fun. The wonderful chronicler of life in French Detroit was Marie Caroline Watson Hamlin. She was also the author of the spooky tales *Legends of Le Detroit*, written near the end of the nineteenth century. Hamlin tells us that Detroit French weddings were usually held at the home of the bride. They began with the bride and the most distinguished guest leading the dancing. Perhaps the important guest was Monsieur Joseph Campau, who in the 1830s was the wealthiest man in Michigan. He was described by the writer George Bates:

> *His greeting was warm and country style. "Bonjour, Monsieur! Comment ça va, Mon Ami?"…clad in a black full dress suit, white cravat, rolling shirt collar, ruffled shirt, clean and white as snow,…with his long white hair, large grey eyes.*

The guests danced "stately minuets" and "graceful cotillions," Fisher's hornpipe and the Reel a' Huit. George Bates, continued:

> *Joseph Campau, Pierre "Papa" Desnoyer, Major Dequindre, majestic Barney Campau, waltzing and frolicking at eighty years of age, with such beautiful girls as Josephine Desnoyer, Anna Dequindre, Mary Williams and all it told of innocent mirth…where age never forgot the joys and pleasures of youth, and where youth always respected, revered and loved old age.*

After the dance, the guests filed into the dining room. Each table setting had a fork and spoon. In the earliest days, the guests carried their own knives, either a jackknife or a dagger suspended from the neck in a sheath of silk or birch bark ornamented with Indian embroidery. The handles were mother of pearl. Drinking goblets were silver and were preserved carefully by families. An aperitif started the repast: brandy for the gents, and a mild cordial for ladies. Following that, the dinner began with soup, the poisson blanc (white fish), poisson dorée (pickerel), pike, roast pig, potatoes, blood pudding, partridges, wild turkey, ragouts, venison larded, pâtés of pommes de terres (potatoes), sagamite (a dish made from ground corn like polenta but

Joseph Campau (1769–1863) was considered the wealthiest man in Michigan in the early nineteenth century. Joseph Campau Street in Detroit, which runs from the river almost to Seven Mile Road, is named after him.

served with milk and maple syrup; Madame Hamlin notes that Charlevoix mentioned sagamite as early as 1722) and, for dessert, praline, galette de beurre (crepes), crocque cignol (a kind of donut), omelette soufflé, floating islands (meringue with caramel), pears, apples and, in summer, grapes. Coffee ended the night.

THE VICTORIAN DINNER

If a dinner—you mustn't say dinner party—is a success, it's the most perfect form of entertainment I know of. If not, it's the most pokey and dismal of failures.
—Detroit society woman, quoted in the Detroit Free Press, *1907*

The dinner was everything during this period. It displayed wealth and refinement, it strengthened one's social connections and standing, it was used to raise money and awareness for charities and it gave rich people a chance to strut.

A Detroit dining room at the turn of the century.

ARRANGING THE TABLE

To be able to throw a dinner party for, say, forty people, the Detroit housewife needed servants, a big dining room and the knowledge of how to set a proper table. As the *Detroit Free Press* advised in 1907:

> *Of course the hostess who has only one or two servants has to spend a lot of time planning, but the woman with an elaborate domestic ménage leaves it all to others.*

Cookbook author and celebrity chef François Tanty offered his "practical hints" to American housewives through his cookbook *Cuisine Française: French Cooking for Every Household, Adapted for American Household*. Chef Tanty knew his stuff. He was trained under Marie-Antoine Carême, the most famous nineteenth-century French chef. He served as chef de cuisine to Emperor Napoleon III and chef to the czar and the imperial family of Russia. In the early 1890s, he came to America to establish his two sons in business. One of his sons, M. Louis Tanty, collaborated on this book and was responsible for the translation. It went through several printings and was very popular in Detroit. The *Detroit Free Press* thought so highly of the book that it had the book published in a special edition, which it offered for sale to Detroit housewives for fifteen cents a copy. Tanty states in his book:

> At first glance nothing pleases the eye of a guest more than a well set table, that is to say, where elegance is combined with good taste. On that matter Americans need very little advice, because, as a rule, they are very fond of fine linen and decorations of fruit and flowers...Candle light being more fashionable than gas, and also more beautifying for the ladies, candelabra should be placed in sufficient number.
>
> Before each plate place the necessary number of glasses, of different sizes, according to the wines that are to be served; this number not to surpass five, viz:
>
> A glass for water.
> A glass for white wine, claret and burgundy.
> A glass for Madeira, sherry and sweet dessert wines.
> A glass for Rhine wine (if served).
> A glass or cup for champagne.

In 1876, the *Detroit Free Press* advised its readers to "allow at least 18 inches at table for each guest...The table linen should be of the whitest, starched and ironed in bias lines to look handsomely upon the table."

Mrs. Mary Henderson was another nationally known authority on entertaining whose column was carried in the Detroit papers. She makes additional suggestions, noting that dishes should be served from the side table:

> Let us suppose a table laid for eight persons, dressed in its best; as attendants, only two persons—a butler and a footman, or one of these, with a page or neat waiting-maid; and let us suppose some one stationed outside the door in the butler's pantry to do nothing but fetch up, or hand, or carry off dishes, one by one:
>
> While guests are being seated, person from outside brings up soup;
> Footman receives soup at door;

Butler serves it out;
Footman hands it;
Both change plates.
Footman takes out soup, and receives fish at door; while butler hands wine;
Butler serves out fish;
Footman hands it (plate in one hand, and sauce in the other);
Both change plates.
Footman brings in entrée, while butler hands wine;
Butler hands entrée;
Footman hands vegetables;
Both change plates,
Etc., etc.

Now we get serious. The following commentary on a Detroit dinner party is from the *Detroit Free Press* of 1876:

Dinner being now ready, it should be announced by the butler or dining-room maid. Never ring a bell for a meal. Bells do very well for country inns and steamboats, but in private houses the ménage should be conducted with as little noise as possible...And now we are ready for the dinner:

The Bill of Fare

First Course
Mock Turtle Soup
Do not give too much, a ladle full is sufficient. It looks gross to give a great deal.

Second Course
Boiled Salmon—*or salmon trout*—
served with egg sauce. Lay a fancily folded napkin on the platter under the well drained fish. Serve the sauce from a sauce tureen.

Third Course
Entrées
Oyster patters, apple fritters—these served with meats and vegetables only on small plates by themselves.

The Roasts are meant to be carved by the host and the vegetables served by the waiters. The roast beef (the "porter house roast" is considered the "choicest" cut), and roast chicken, vegetables, at least four kinds, mashed potatoes…Have fancy pickles on the table and raw, ripe sliced tomatoes garnished with parsley

Fourth Course
Game in its season with which currant jelly should be served.

Fifth Course
Salads. Of course any dishes used and no longer needed should be removed between each course, the table brushed and made tidy by the waiter for the next course.

Sixth Course
Desserts. In a private house [desserts] are supposed to be served by the host and hostess from either end of the table. We will have lemon meringue, ice cream, gold and silver cake, fruit, confectionary, and French coffee, the last strong and clear, with no milk or sugar, and served in small French cups.

BREAKFAST, LUNCH AND BIRTHDAY PARTIES

During the Victorian era, Detroiters begin to have children's parties, breakfast gatherings, luncheons and suppers; at that time, supper was considered a secondary, late evening meal lighter than dinner.

Several cookbook authors offer menus for breakfast parties that include oranges dressed with a fork and diamonds of ham. Of course, you must have pancakes and a bottle of Chateau d'Yquem White Bordeaux wine, which is currently worth about $10,000 a case. (The years 1847 and 1859 are listed as two of the best six vintages ever produced at Yquem.)

A, skewer; B, slices of truffles; C, mushrooms.

An illustration from the book *Hand-book of Practical Cookery for Ladies and Professional Cooks* by French chef Pierre Blot. *Special Collections, Michigan State University Libraries.*

Early Spring Breakfast

1st Course.—An Havana orange for each person, dressed on a fork.

2d Course.—Boiled shad, maître d'hôtel sauce; Saratoga potatoes. Tea or coffee.

3d Course.—Lamb-chops, tomato sauce. (Château Yquem).

4th Course.—Omelet, with green pease, or garnished with parsley and thin diamonds of ham, or with shrimps, etc., etc.

5th Course.—Fillets of beef, garnished with water-cresses and little round radishes; muffins.

6th Course.—Pancakes with maple syrup.

Then there are the kids—don't forget the tongue sandwiches! In 1880, the following menu was syndicated across the United States and in Detroit by cooking expert Maria Parola, who toured the nation, stopping in Detroit several times to give cooking classes:

CHILDREN'S PARTY FOR FIFTY

Chicken Sandwiches.
Tongue Sandwiches.
Buttered Rolls.
Buttered Slices of Bread.
Richmond Maids of Honor.
Gâteau St. Honoré [a cake].
Dominos.

and other Small Cakes.
Vanilla and Chocolate Ice Cream.
Candies and Fruit.

The meat for the sandwiches should be chopped fine. The rolls must be small, and the buttered bread should be cut in thin slices, two slices be put together, and then be cut into long strips or little squares. There should be one hundred sandwiches, seventy-five rolls, one hundred slices of bread, forty maids of honor, six dishes of gâteau St. Honoré, two gallons of each kind of ice cream, and a generous supply of small cakes, candies and fruit.

THE ETIQUETTE OF CARVING THE ROAST

Everyone sits down to eat, but the roast must be carved by the man of the house. Proper carving at the dinner table was a complicated yet artful skill in 1852, especially if you were serving a calf's head:

Calf's Head—There is much more meat to be obtained from a calf's head by carving it one way than another. Carve from A to B, cutting quite down to the bone. At the fleshy part of the neck you will find the throat sweetbread, which you can help a slice of with the other part; you will remove the eye with the point of the knife and divide it in half, helping those to it who profess a preference for it; there are some tasty, gelatinous pieces around it which are palatable. Remove the jaw-bone, and then you will find meat with some fine flavored lean; the palate, which is under the head, is by some thought a dainty, and should be proffered when carving.

Of course, not every dinner party goes as planned: "To begin with the tablecloth was on crooked and the center piece would have looked better in the wash."

Then there's your husband's useless brother, as in this excerpt from the *Detroit Free Press* in 1891:

Nothing is more enlivening when the guests are discussing dessert than a well-selected series of tricks…An amusing trick is to place three or four water glasses in a row. Then another on top of that and so on until a pyramid with a single glass on top is formed. Now invite your neighbor to fill the top glass with water, then the two supporting it and so on. Chances are…he will make a slip and topple the whole pyramid over. This never fails to promote much merriment and also provoke the host and hostess but as you will never be invited to another dinner, what do you care?

Or that clueless young business partner, as in this 1906 *Detroit Free Press* article:

The salad looked first rate as salads go…this one was pretty and garnished with three healthy nasturtium blooms…Selecting two of the blooms I proceeded to put them in my button hole. My wife reached over and pinched me. "What are you doing?" my wife whispered severely.
"I'm putting on my boutonnière."
"That isn't a boutonnière! It's your salad."

And then, there is always your husband to ruin everything:

Her husband bends over his soup plate until his beard almost dips into the soup, and from the time of lifting the first soup spoon to his lips until the last drop is drained makes a noise akin to that of a sawmill!

3

Christmas in Old Detroit

Celebrations of Christmas in Detroit over the centuries have been highlighted by feasts and charity, toys and trees—and fires caused by lighted candles on those trees. Although Protestant churches in Detroit did not embrace the Christmas holiday until the 1840s, it was long celebrated in the French Catholic churches, such as Detroit's oldest parish, St. Anne's.

Before Christmas trees became the rage, the French holiday tradition in Detroit was represented by Yule logs, réveillon feasting and horse races. Yule logs were enormous logs or sometimes entire tree stumps that filled the hearth, along with a half cord of wood to get them started. Holiday feasting began on Christmas Eve in a tradition called réveillon (pronounced ray-veh-yon), which is still celebrated in Quebec and New Orleans (at least for the tourists).

In Detroit, families would carry a lantern to midnight mass and leave it with a beggar at the church door. When the Christmas mass was over, they would pick up their lantern and give a Christmas tip to the beggar. They then would go home for the feast, which would last until 8:00 a.m. The réveillon supper was a sumptuous menu that included la tourtière—a meat pie made with pigeons in the nineteenth century and later with pork, veal or other game. Other dishes might include a stew of meatballs and pork, minced pork pie, turkey, pumpkin pie, mince pie and new cider. If turkeys were available, they were cleaned, seasoned, suspended from a cord over the hearth fire and then slowly turned and basted. They were wild turkeys and

A group of Detroiters out celebrating New Years Eve in the 1940s.

not nearly as big as current birds. "Too much for one, not enough for two" was a quote recorded by city historian Friend Palmer in his book *Early Days in Detroit*.

The men raced their French ponies up Michigan Avenue when there was snow. In 1851, Ulysses S. Grant was a lieutenant stationed in Detroit after the Mexican War. He was frequently seen racing horses during the holiday on the streets or on the frozen Detroit River. In the French homes, small gifts for children were put in shoes. Indians were also welcomed and exchanged gifts and food with Detroiters on both Christmas and New Year's Day. Prominent early Detroiters Joseph Campau, Antoine Dequindre and Peter Desnoyer were among the generous contributors to the festivities of the day.

On the Town

Ho-Ho-Hotel

Much later in Victorian days, Detroit hotels competed for locals, and it became a custom for Detroiters to enjoy their holiday dinners at hotel restaurants. The following is the bill of fare from the famed Russell House Hotel in 1888. The meal was enjoyed with rousing Christmas music from the Russell House Orchestra:

Mill Po. oysters on the half shell
Green turtle
Chicken
Kennebec salmon broiled à la maître de hotel
Filet of beef larded with fresh mushrooms
Sweetbreads braised with French peas
Pineapple fritters, glace a maraschino
Roman punch
Christmas beef with horseradish
Turkey stuffed with chestnuts
Cranberry sauce
Hubbard squash. Green peas. Sweet potatoes.
Chicken salad. Boned turkey in aspic. Pâté fois gras.
Currant jelly. Apple jelly. Apple butter.
Prairie hen. Mallard duck. Partridge. Quail.
Cauliflower. Boiled potatoes. String beans.
Christmas pudding. Brandy sauce.
Apple pie. Mince pie.
Fruit cake. Angel food. Charlotte Russe.
Madeira jelly. Tutti frutti ice cream.
Fruits.
Roquefort. Stilton. Pineapple cheese.
Bent crackers. Coffee.

FIRE HAZARDS

The hotel most likely had a Christmas tree, which was becoming a tradition in the later half of the nineteenth century. Prior to electric tree lights, people used candles. They were attached to the tree using melted wax, glue, special pins or small metal cups. People also put candles on wreaths and roping.

Open flames on a real Christmas tree was perhaps the most dangerous Christmas idea ever conceived, especially when the tree began to dry out. On top of this, people decorated the floor beneath the tree with cotton batting sprinkled with silver-colored confetti to look like snow. Sometimes they surrounded the candles with cotton sprinkled with sugar to make it look like snow on the tree. It was popular to use highly combustible, sometimes exploding, ornaments made from aniline dye, discovered in 1856, which produced a rich purple color. These also produced toxic fumes when burning. Celluloid ornaments were popular, as well, and also extremely flammable. On top of this, many homes from the Civil War until the twentieth century were lit with gas. The gas lighting system was done through thin pipes that came out from the wall about one foot and angled upward. At the pipe's end was a jet nozzle, which emitted an open flame. Families loved to loop pine roping around the pipes of the gas jets. Once the tree was lit, the gaslight was turned down for dramatic effect; then, after experiencing the beauty of the Christmas tree lit with candles in a darkened room, the gas was cranked way up to bathe the room in bright light and "capture the spirit of Christmas"—and occasionally catch the roping on fire. Disasters were inevitable, as these reports from Detroit newspapers indicate:

> *1902: 213 East Palmer Street was damaged to the extent of $200 by fire at five o'clock yesterday afternoon. The blaze was caused by a Christmas tree catching fire from a candle.*

> *1902: A Christmas tree loaded with inflammable ornaments and candles caused a six story building to burn down the Alexander Student building.*

> *1904: A false beard worn by Burritt M. Tuttle, judge of the town court, who was enacting the part of Santa Claus at the Christmas Celebration at the Methodist Church, caught fire from the Christmas tree candles and Judge Tuttle was severely burned. The church was threatened by fire and a panic was prevented with great difficulty.*

Holiday decorating had grown so dangerous that it became an annual Christmas tradition for the Detroit fire marshal to issue fire warnings about trees.

In 1909, Detroit fire chief James Broderick summed up his views succinctly: "Don't have a Christmas tree at all!...The worst of it is they go up like tinder once they get a good start."

THE FIRST CHRISTMAS TREE LIGHTS

The first known electrically illuminated Christmas tree was the creation of Edward H. Johnson, an associate of inventor Thomas Edison. While he was vice-president of the Edison Electric Light Co., he had Christmas tree light bulbs made especially for him. He proudly displayed his Christmas tree, which was hand wired with eighty red, white and blue electric incandescent light bulbs the size of walnuts, on December 22, 1882, at his home on Fifth Avenue in New York City. Local New York newspapers ignored the story, seeing it as a publicity stunt. However, it was published by a Detroit newspaper, and the rest of the nation picked up on it. Johnson became widely regarded as the father of electric Christmas tree lights.

Electric lights on trees did not become widespread until the 1930s. Giant municipal Christmas trees appeared because electric lights made them possible. Detroit's first municipal tree appeared in 1912, ordered by Mayor Oscar Marx. It was set up on Woodward Avenue opposite city hall, and the tradition for three years was to have Mayor Marx's son Junior throw the switch to light up the tree.

Finding a Christmas tree in Detroit in the nineteenth century wasn't always easy. Forest fires had ravaged landscapes, and harvesting trees in big quantities on reforested land was restricted. This led to an enterprising idea by Detroit businessman G.S. Ferguson in 1909: a Christmas tree farm. He formed the Evergreen Tree Company and planted fir trees in Alcona County near Lake Huron on eighty acres of land.

His initial reason for doing so was not to grow and sell Christmas trees. On a trip to Paris in 1900, he had learned that a Parisian pharmaceutical company would pay sixteen dollars a pound for evergreen fir sap. It was later that he began getting requests from around the United States for small trees

An unknown girl has her picture taken with Santa Claus at Kern's Department Store, 1940s. *Author's collection.*

for Christmas. Business was so good that he immediately expanded from eighty to six hundred acres. He claimed he could never meet demand and encouraged others to open Christmas tree farms. Demand for Christmas trees grew every year, especially at the start of the twentieth century. In 1908, fifteen thousand trees were reported sold; in 1910, thirty thousand; and in 1912, Detroiters bought seventy-five thousand trees. At that time, Detroiters preferred spruce trees to pines.

FROM WOODEN TOYS TO RIFLES

Then, as now, the charm of Christmas came from children. The earliest purchased Christmas toys were described as sugar roosters, gingerbread horses or Indians and bobsleds. By the 1840s, Detroit stores were advertising wooden toys for boys, such as wooden guns, sabers, rocking horses, whips, soldiers with gold helmets and toy horses with real manes. Girls had dolls advertised in the paper with "white satin robes, real shoes, genuine hair, round faces, snow white cheeks touched with spots of red, pinched up mouths, and large blue eyes."

By 1882, toy kitchens were marketed with something new: a tin stove. Boys could get locomotives, toy velocipedes (bicycles) and the usual guns, knives, whips, swords and cannons. Toys and soldier uniforms corresponded to the current conflict, so in 1899, it was the Spanish-American War. One toy was a cannon that shot rubber balls at a Spanish fort; when the fort was hit, a waving American flag sprung up.

By 1892, toys had become more mechanical, at least for boys: iron toy banks, wind-up painted tin toys of monkeys churning butter, slithering snakes, tricycle-riding Uncle Sam and a wind-up naphtha launch, which was a toy version of a nationally popular, ultra-modern, aluminum-body sailboat.

In 1902, batteries that lasted six months drove a new toy that began to appear: toy automobiles. There were battery-driven farmyard chickens that really pecked grain, flying vessels (no airplanes yet—the Wright brothers' first flight was in 1903), soldiers dressed like Rough Riders and a new game based on the Boer War. Boys could get "miniature rifles that shoot real bullets to bring down sparrows," which perhaps might have given birth to the parental admonishment, "You'll put somebody's eye out."

A group of boys in a Detroit Department of Recreation class make Christmas toys for orphanages and hospitals in the 1930s. *Author's collection.*

WINDOW DISPLAYS

Christmas store displays of toys and adult gifts could be magnificent. One unique Christmas display at Edward W. Alexander's umbrella shop on Monroe Street featured umbrellas surrounded by pretty plants, colored lights and live alligators. In December 1890, J.L. Hudson's advertised: "Silk and bowler hats for the gents, and for the ladies fur muffs in black lynx, natural lynx, Japanese monkey, opossum, beaver, or cape seal."

Shoppers crowded downtown streets in the tens of thousands in the 1900s. The large department stores on Woodward Avenue were mobbed to capacity. In 1903, it was necessary to wait in line to even get into the stores.

On the Town

A Tradition of Giving

Nothing captures the spirit of Christmas in Detroit better than the virtue of generosity. Detroiters annually supplied dinners, presents and good cheer for thousands of people, such as a dinner for two to three hundred wounded Civil War soldiers convalescing in Detroit in 1863, as reported in the *Detroit Free Press*:

> *The Christmas Dinner given to invalid soldiers at Fireman's Hall was in all respects a success…the old and established character of the citizens did not fail in this emergency; enough and more was brought in with tables loaded with luxuries which usually abound on those of first class hotels…The Detroit City Band furnished the music for the occasion. The good old air of Yankee Doodle was played and caused visible commotion among the feet of the guests making even the cripples and crutches keep time to its lively notes….Not even those [soldiers] whose [tendency] to sin brought them to the guard house were omitted from the festivities… Both the giver and receiver are equally blessed.*

In 1881, more than six thousand Christmas dinners were served. Christmas dinner for two thousand people was served in Cadillac Square in 1899. Men at the Detroit House of Corrections and Wayne County Jail and two hundred men at the McGregor Mission on Brush Street got Christmas dinners in 1902. Campfire girls provided dinner and gifts for two hundred children younger than eight years old in 1921.

The Old Newsboys' Goodfellow Fund was started in 1914 by James J. Brady with the sole mission of bringing Christmas to poor children. Brady, along with about three hundred Detroit businessmen, sold newspapers on street corners to raise money to purchase gifts for kids. By 1922, the Goodfellows were serving more than seventeen thousand children with food, baseballs, dolls, infant nursery needs, gloves, mittens and more. Other civic organizations also contributed food baskets, clothing, Christmas parties and Santas. The total number of people taken care of in 1922 was thirty-five thousand.

In some years, three tons of coal was handed out in small amounts to go along with dinner gift baskets so that people had a way to cook their dinners once they got them home. Shoes, stockings and underwear were regularly given out, along with toys, to children. The tradition continues today.

The notion of helping and sharing was deeply ingrained, as this 1847 newspaper exhortation indicates:

> *You that delight in doing good—and who is there that should not—search out a destitute family and by the small donation of a turkey, pig or some such thing make a "Merry Christmas" for those who otherwise would return to their beds hungry and starving.*

PART II
WORKING FOR A LIVING

4

To Market, To Market

Saturday Morning at the Market

As spring turns to summer in Detroit, thousands of people head to the Eastern Market on Saturday mornings to stroll and shop. The Detroit Eastern Market began as a hay market and wood yard and then, in the 1890s, became a farmers' market. It has always been popular, but it was one of only three markets at the turn of the century. The Western Market was located at Michigan Avenue and Trumbull, while the Central Market took up Cadillac Square in front of Detroit's old city hall. The Eastern Market was one of a series of public markets that stretch back to Detroit's beginnings.

The City of Detroit owned the market and derived income from stall rentals and charging farmers selling vegetables and flowers from wagons. Just as now, Saturday was the day when things happened. Friday was the worst day to go "marketing" since it was a well-known fact that farmers saved their best produce for Saturday. During the week in 1899, about five to six thousand people per day went to the Eastern Market, while Saturdays drew between thirteen and fifteen thousand customers.

Cadillac Square Market in Detroit, circa 1890. *George Washington Merrill Photograph Collection (bl003974), Bentley Historical Library, University of Michigan.*

Before 8:00 a.m., the market was filled with peddlers and grocers stocking up, but after 8:00 a.m. the housewives arrived. Many pushed baby carriages, which they used to carry heavy vegetables home à la early shopping carts. So many baby carriages clogged the aisles that the market committee passed an ordinance forbidding baby carriages with no babies in them in the open-air buildings or "sheds." The next week, baby carriages suddenly had babies; as described in the papers, "Sometimes there would be but a bald, little head protruding among the cabbages."

At this time, immigrants were coming to Detroit by the thousands, and each nationality shopped on a separate day at the Eastern Market. Eastside Jews came on one day, and Polish ladies brought their husbands on another. German *hausfraus* were considered very independent, and Belgians were described as "close buyers but good customers."

Hungarians took trains from Milwaukee Junction. Italians and Syrians came another day from "streets by the river." They all came to save a penny or two, as the market had the cheapest prices in town; the stall keepers knew what each nationality wanted and therefore what to put on sale.

The Central Market was the pride of Detroit when it opened and attracted a wealthier clientele. It was three hundred feet long and rivaled markets in Boston, New York and Philadelphia. In 1899, ladies would roll up to the market in coaches and carriages with drivers in livery; the poor walked. In 1909, the well-to-do women motored to the market in a Detroit Electric Vehicle or were "whirled there by a chauffeur."

The market was open all day and into the night. Initially, it was lit by "penny candles." They were replaced by gaslights, and in 1882 electric lights were turned on: "The cluster of ten electric lights were in operation for the first time last night and gave a very brilliant light, which was viewed by a large number of citizens."

Heat was provided in 1880 by stoves—Detroit's own Crown Jewel baseburners, which were later replaced by steam pipes.

Markets sold more than vegetables. In fact, many vegetable stall keepers were farmers, considered second-class citizens. A few were described as "queer looking old-fellows with unkempt heads and beards that grow after peculiar patterns and fashions none but a country man could devise." Vegetable stalls were open-air wooden structures. In the markets, the real heavies were the butchers. In 1883, the old City Hall Market had sixteen stalls for butchers. Butchers were substantial businessmen with investments in cutting blocks, knives and equipment, iceboxes, carcass hooks and meat. Many purchased live animals and pastured them in the country on farms they owned, bringing them to market when needed. A few butchers, like William Smith, also owned slaughtering and meatpacking facilities. In Detroit, Germans were prominent in the profession and belonged to the German Butchers and Drovers Association. They had political clout; butchers were elected as aldermen on the Detroit Common Council. In the 1880s, the butchers at different markets challenged one another to baseball games, gave meat to the poor and raised money for charities. Throughout the Midwest, butchers competed in butchering and meat dressing competitions attended by hundreds of fans. The national champion was from Indianapolis. They were big powerful men described by one as "Hercules with a slight paunch."

Markets later sold fish and oysters shipped in from the East. The delay for including fish stalls was based on the rank smell from unwashed wooden fish "benches" used to scale and gut fish. To address this and general sanitation at the Central Market, a sewer was built under the market with sewer pipes running to the butcher stalls and fish benches so that they could be washed clean and properly drained.

Services such as woodcutting could be procured, and even dry goods, such as clothing, shoes and umbrellas, were sold. In 1889, the *Detroit Free Press* wrote:

> *A man whose shoulders and arms were literally buried beneath a load of suspenders stood in front of the Central Market building at around 7 o'clock last evening. The suspenders were of the most radiant hues including every color in the rainbow.*

THE EARLY DETROIT MARKETS

In the early days of the nineteenth century, there was a market at Jefferson just west of Woodward Avenue. This was followed by the Berthelet Market at the corner of Randolph and Atwater (currently the Renaissance Center), which lasted until 1848, when it burned. Fruits and vegetables were brought to the market by French wives and daughters from Detroit and Canada who maintained farm gardens.

A famous English novelist of the day, Mrs. Anna Jameson, visited Detroit in 1838 and wrote the following observations in her book *Winter Studies and Summer Rambles in Canada* as she crossed the Detroit River by ferry to Windsor:

> *A pretty little steamer, gaily painted, with streamers flying, and shaded by an awning, is continually passing and re-passing from shore to shore. I have sometimes sat in this ferry-boat for a couple of hours together…amused, meantime, by the variety and conversation of the passengers, English emigrants, and French Canadians; brisk Americans; dark, sad-looking Indians folded in their blankets; farmers, storekeepers, speculators in wheat; artisans; trim girls with black eyes and short petticoats, speaking a Norman patois, and bring baskets of fruit to the Detroit market.*

A market butcher, circa 1868, from *The Market Assistant* by Thomas Farrington DeVoe. *Special Collections, Michigan State University Libraries.*

French wives and farmers brought produce on their unique two-wheeled carts, open in the back, pulled by shaggy ponies. The carts, called *charettes*, would also take people to church, gatherings or markets down the narrow streets, sometimes only ten feet wide and clogged with mud. The French orchards on the Detroit side of the river were known for exceptional apples, such as the Caville Red, Snow Apple and the "Detroit Red," for both eating and cider. They maintained glorious pear trees that rose sixty feet from seeds said to have originated in France. The French wives and girls would sit in front of the market before Jefferson Avenue on a stone slab scrubbed clean, with their baskets of produce for sale. Others brought eggs, geese, butter and more.

Here was a place of noise, smells, food, children, gossip, Native Americans, farmers, frontiersmen, fishermen, shouting, hawking and laughing. The disreputable and the reputable could be found; in front of the market was the sheriff's whipping post for those who had trouble following the rules. It also included great numbers of visiting French Canadian voyageurs, fur trappers and more—everybody selling or looking for bargains.

At this time in Detroit, people used maple sugar everyday, while white cane sugar was a luxury saved for special occasions. Maple sugar was made by the Ojibwas on the Great Lakes and the Wyandots of the Detroit River and brought to market in birch-bark *mococks*, which held from 50 pounds to only a few ounces. The smallest of these were given to children as candy. In 1819, 150,000 pounds of maple sugar were produced in Michigan. Detroit historian Silas Farmer reported that in 1828, one merchant in Detroit advertised 40,000 pounds of maple sugar for sale. To make sugar, Native Americans gradually reduced the sap to syrup by repeatedly boiling and then freezing it, discarding the ice and starting again. Curiously, children and others who ate the maple sugar had to watch for the tiny bones of fish and small animals, while those who bought the large mococks found the bones of dogs and deer; as they reduced the syrup to sugar, the Ojibwa were known to cook their dinners in the boiling syrup.

Among the most popular items sold at the City Hall Market was wild game, which arrived from all corners of the region via professional hunters and collectors. Since the eastern United States was hunted out by this time, Michigan and Detroit became major suppliers of wild game to New York and Boston via the Erie Canal. Typically, venison, boar or wild birds were served throughout the nineteenth century as a separate course in a dinner party or at holidays.

Vegetable Warfare

Of course, nothing ran perfectly smooth at the early markets; carts flipped over by ponies out of control, whiskey was in abundance and there were the occasional disputes between stall keepers and producers, as was reported by the Detroit newspapers in 1861:

The Cucumber War
Elizabeth...arrived in town seated upon a two wheeled cart loaded with cucumbers, the whole affair propelled by a shagbark pony of French extraction. Elizabeth struck up a trade with Mrs. King a retailer of green groceries and a pugnacious little lady pluck full of ginger and always keeping an eye out for a muss. A little dispute sprang up as to the number of cucumbers...and thereupon they waxed warm...Mrs. King gave her opponent a crack that closed up the left eye...Just as Elizabeth was jamming a cucumber down Mrs. King's throat, her husband joined in. "Yer have the law, at her, bite her, the auld Dutch vagabond."

Under the encouragement they did wonders...all the vendors rushed into the contest...The stalls were cleared of vegetables to serve as missiles; cucumbers filled the air and the combatants grew gory from the effects of smashed beets.

Stall Keepers

Stall keepers took great pride in the appearance of their stalls and the market in general. At the opening of the Mansfield Market on Michigan Grand Avenue in 1878, the main aisle was spectacularly draped with American flags and bunting, while columns were entwined with evergreens. On either side of the stalls were vessels heavy with fruits, flowers, vegetables and all known luxuries of the banquet table. To

A farmer at a Michigan market in the 1930s. *U.S. Library of Congress.*

the right of the entrance, a butcher, Charles Hull, displayed fresh and prepared meats trimmed in floral designs, while upon the counter were displayed his silver and gold medals, cups and other trophies awarded by state and county fairs.

A maddening problem for stall keepers was "sampling," which was a form of friendly stealing but never called that. Everybody took samples: customers, cops, children and neighboring stall keepers. Some vendors reported losing $200 a year from people sampling their goods. Actual stealing was more serious, as stall keepers might watch wheels of cheese or whole carcasses of hogs flying down the aisle ways.

On the other side of the issue, stall keepers were no angels. To make sure stall keepers stayed honest, there were the market clerks, who were appointed by the Detroit Common Council. The clerks collected stall rents, ensured that the market remained clean and wholesome and, with inspectors and police, generally managed the market. They checked weights and measures to ensure that good weight was given. They inspected sacks of flour or coffee for stones or iron filings placed at the bottom to add weight. They watched for "bob" veal—veal sold too young. They kept a lookout for "forestalling" by hucksters—preselling goods before customers reached the stalls to avoid market fees or to resell in the market for a higher price. They watched for pickpockets, who were common on Saturdays:

> *Shortly after 11 o'clock forenoon Mrs. Minnock and her little daughter entered the Central Market. When her little girl asked her to buy a peach Mrs. Minnock put her hand toward her pocket...in doing so she touched the hand of Ernst Meyers who had his hand on her pocket book...Meyers immediately ran into the arms of Officer Shepard.*

FRANCIS BENSON, CENTRAL MARKET TERROR

At times, there were more serious crimes. One man in particular stood out: Francis Benson, the Central Market Terror. Benson—or, as he was called by the papers, "Lord Benson"—was a stall owner who sold vegetables at the market starting in the 1860s with his fiancée and, unfortunately, later his wife. He was immediately considered a troublemaker and, as reported in the Detroit newspapers, was arrested over twenty-five times over the next twenty years, including a charge of manslaughter in the death of his wife, for which he was acquitted. (It was deemed she died of alcohol poisoning, not his violent beating.) He was arrested for every conceivable offense at the market, including assault, abusive language, disturbing the peace, punching a market clerk, false weights on blueberries, drunkenness, obnoxious behavior, indecent exposure, shooting his pistol into a crowd and "acting insane." (He probably didn't know it was a crime.)

Stall keepers typically bought their vegetables from farmers or gardeners who came to the city. However, meat was handled differently. Since refrigerated rail cars were not yet available, cattle, oxen, sheep and hogs—basically, most domestic animals—were driven on the hoof in herds through the city streets, where they were purchased by butchers who then led them to the neighborhood slaughterhouse or slaughtered them in their stalls.

In Detroit, most meat began as livestock at the King's Drovers or Cattle Yards on Grand River at Second Avenue, then on the outskirts of the city at the former farm of Lewis Cass. Cattle arrived from the country to be held at King's in pens. A drover would buy a small herd—a drove—between ten and forty animals and begin the slow walk to Detroit. It took several days. The drover team consisted of a boss, who rode a horse; a crew, who walked; and their dogs. Teams would stop for the night to eat and sleep at inns along the road that were equipped with separated corrals and feed to hold their cattle or hogs for the night. Drovers could be a crude bunch. They arrived from afternoon until nine o'clock at night, pounding on the table to demand food—and a lot of it—and shots of bitters or whiskey. After a short night's sleep, they were back on the road, with teams leaving from three o'clock the following morning until nearly noon. Innkeepers and their families worked the exhausting pace nonstop and also served stagecoaches and farmer's wagons.

Whether you called it a slaughterhouse or the less graphic, more genteel French term *abattoir*, the killing and butchering of animals occurred on the streets in the early days of Detroit. Most Detroiters did their best to walk around these places. Detroit's City Hall Market was no exception. The butchers would select live animals, have them slaughtered and then cart the meat to their stalls or shops. It was these slaughterhouses, found in all the bigger cities of the United States, that were dangerous, disgusting and appropriately loathed. These slaughtering areas (formerly known as open-air "shambles") prompted the Detroit mayor and aldermen to pass a regulation that forbade "private" slaughtering of animals; all animals had to be slaughtered at the market only and not in the neighborhoods or alleyways of Detroit.

A *New York Times* editorial in 1865 summed up the public's love affair with slaughterhouses:

> *Of all the offences against public health and decency which are perpetrated in this great city, there is none more gross and abominable, more pregnant with deadly and debasing consequences, than the maintenance, within the city proper, of those establishments... passerby invariably slipping and sliding in the foul compound which floods the way...The pen is disgusting in the extreme. Portions of animal remains, straw, excrements, filth of almost every description,*

all mingled into a hideous mass, at all seasons, exude a pestilential
stench. It is impossible adequately to describe this place of horrors.
The moans of the poor brutes can be distinctly heard for a long
distance, and the whole affair is pitiable in one aspect and utterly
disgraceful in all.

By the late 1860s, livestock was important industry to Michigan, with
more hogs sold than cattle; cattle came from Chicago. Michigan farmers
produced nearly half a million hogs, and drovers handled most since
shipping "dressed" hogs or carcasses in the early days of rail cars produced
high losses due to spoilage. As street slaughtering ended, Detroit relied on
established slaughtering enterprises. In the 1860s, the oldest and biggest
slaughterhouse was owned by John Bigley. It was located one mile south
of the city on the Detroit River and was considered humane and efficient.
Bigley got no pay for his work but took the remains of the animals, for
which the owners had no use, and sold them to candle factories. Finished
carcasses from Bigley (hogs, sheep and some cattle) were taken by wagons
to meatpackers in the city who prepared them into cuts of meat sold to
grocers, restaurants and butchers in the market. Many were shipped to
lumbering camps up north.

By 1915, Detroit meatpackers had earned an international reputation
for excellence in bacon, ham and even beef rib roasts. While a small
fraction of Chicago's output, Detroit packers earned revenues of
$30,000,000 and employed 3,500 men to become one of the city's biggest
industries of the day. In London, England, Detroit hams were eagerly
sought after.

Eventually, markets grow old. The Central Market, which was the
pride of Detroit, simply wore out and was a dilapidated wreck by 1891.
It needed to be closed. The Central Market was in the center of the
city at that time. The press pulled no punches in 1892 to get the old
building demolished to make way for a grassy square with fountains
and benches:

A VERITABLE BARNACLE
…Our experience with the central market building. It was an
architectural monstrosity from the outset and has been a repulsive
blemish on the city ever since…it is causing what should be one of the
handsomest and attractive portions of the city for years to remain an
eyesore and a disgrace. It has depreciated the value of all contiguous

property…It is reeking with grease, filth, bad air and worse odors. It defaces the heart of the city…every vestige of the rat paradise should be removed.

THE MARKET THAT WOULDN'T DIE

In early 1892, the common council voted twenty-four to five to abolish the market in July when the last municipal bond had been redeemed and the debt was cleared. Five aldermen who voted "nay" owned stalls in the market. Especially prickly was alderman William B. Thompson, of the west side eighth ward, who was a butcher in the market. He and the other butchers didn't care what was voted; they were not leaving. July came, and the city abolished the market, but nothing changed. People still arrived with their baskets on Saturday, and the butchers refused to budge. They stopped paying rent. They were now "squatters." The city stopped janitorial service and stopped buying sawdust for the floor. Butchers paid for it themselves. The city cut off heat and lights. The butchers had lights and steam pipes reinstalled. The common council was in an uproar. Christmas came, and the butchers had the "abolished" market decorated. However, in a clever move, the city changed the authority of the market from the common council's market committee to the Department of Public Works; it would tear the building down over their heads. In 1893, a board member of the Department of Public Works, Jake Guthard, entered the building on a Saturday and confronted the butchers. Alderman Thompson, standing before the others, blocked his way. Guthard told them that the building was coming down.

Alderman Thompson answered firmly, "It is not."

Another butcher, Larry Fitzgerald, brought out his cleaver and swung it at Guthard, then chased him out of the building as the other butchers laughed heartily. Thompson and another alderman, Beck, mocked Guthard when he complained of his treatment at the next meeting of the common council, the papers reported.

The butchers filed an injunction to stop the demolition. It went to the state Supreme Court, which ruled in favor of the city: the butchers had to go. In the meantime, the market was growing nastier by the week, with tramps loitering about and rats becoming a growing menace. The butchers began posting guards to warn them of sneak attacks or night raids. They

Farmers with their vegetables at a Michigan produce market, 1930s. *U.S. Library of Congress.*

held their cleavers and knives at the ready in case the police showed up. Nobody was eager to make a move.

Jake Guthard and board members of the Department of Public Works were feeling the pressure.

"What are you going to do about that infernal old market?" aldermen and reporters demanded to know.

They decided to hire a new secretary, who would be responsible for ridding the market of the butchers. His name was Andrew McPherson. He was very young and had been an enthusiastic sidewalk inspector. The board promoted him for "his enthusiasm."

Secretary McPherson took on the job. Since the butchers would never be persuaded into moving, McPherson and the board decided to sell the large oak walk-in ice cabinets that the butchers used to store their meat. The cabinets were city property.

On February 4, 1894, a Saturday night, McPherson entered the market to inform the butchers of the plan. The market was active with shoppers, mainly elderly patrons who had been coming for decades.

Alderman Thompson was in his stall.

"Good Evening, Alderman," said McPherson.

"Hello, Mac," replied Thompson. "The boy from the eighth [ward]."

"I have an unpleasant duty to perform," the secretary said reluctantly.

"Well, what is it? I'm ready for anything," the alderman laughed.

"The board has sold those iceboxes. And at four o'clock Monday morning, the purchaser will be here to remove his property."

"That's a good one," Thompson replied, laughing again.

Another of the butchers said, "I guess we'd better sell all our meat today, then."

McPherson walked up to each stall and repeated to each butcher that the walk-in iceboxes had been sold and would be taken out. Larry Fitzgerald set his cleaver in clear view.

McPherson made arrangements with the new owner of the iceboxes, S.B. Dixon, to meet him at 4:00 a.m. at the market to dismantle the boxes and take them out. Along with Dixon's assistants, he brought a squad of policemen. McPherson waited alone in the dark on a cold Sunday morning, watching the butchers' guards. At 4:30 a.m., Sam Dixon and his crew arrived, as did the police. McPherson went up to the guard who blocked their way holding a weapon.

"You can't go in," the guard said.

As planned, McPherson distracted him while Dixon's crew took a heavy wood extension ladder and smashed it, battering ram style though the door. All rushed in as the guards took off to notify the butchers. Dixon's men began dismantling the iceboxes quickly. McPherson had wagons brought along and had the meat put on the wagons.

Armed butchers burst into the market "hopping mad." Larry Fitzgerald was the first one in with his infamous cleaver, but Alderman Thompson held him back.

"That's it, boys," he said calmly. "Pack up your duds and tote your meat across the street to the new place."

They had a new location already set up and were all out of the market before noon. The showdown was over.

Working for a Living

An 1894 editorial from the *Detroit Free Press* stated the next day:

> *Old residents clung to the central market as a sacred reminder of the past and defended it as a vested right. The butchers hung on like grim death because there was money in it...The board of public works was never more in earnest in the history of its organization...But alas for the butchers and joy for everyone else in Detroit.*

5

The Milk Peddlers' War

Before gallon jugs of milk, before yogurt sticks, chocolate milk, nondairy creamers, even before milkmen, there were the milk peddlers. The milk peddlers—both men and women—numbered in the hundreds in Detroit and were common throughout cities of Michigan from before the Civil War until about 1920. According to the *Detroit Free Press* in 1875:

> *Mrs. Gertrude Klinck is a milk peddler, and yesterday she left her horse wagon and cans on Russell Street while she entered a grocery store to make some purchases. She desires to know now where her horse and wagon are.*

They delivered on foot or rode their horse-drawn wagons up streets selling milk out of cans, ladling it into customers' pitcher. The larger peddlers, called "dealers," had multiple wagons and hired deliverymen. They included companies such as Towar Creamery, A. Easter, Union Creamery and more, which also delivered wholesale to restaurants, ice cream parlors—like Sanders—and grocers. Many peddlers owned their own cows. Unlike trusted milkmen in their trucks, milk peddlers had a decidedly mixed reputation: colorful, cantankerous, independent, distrusted and sometimes even crazy. They were pursued relentlessly by city milk and sanitary inspectors such as the merciless Dr. William H. Price.

Milk peddlers appeared in Detroit before the Civil War. Prior to that, 93 percent of Americans lived on farms and had their own milk cows, or a neighbor with one, and usually bartered for a pitcher of milk. There was no such thing as a dairy industry. But times were changing. Approximately 45,000 people lived in Detroit in the 1860s. As the twentieth century began, Detroit was sitting pretty. The population roared ahead: Wayne County had 119,054 people in 1870. By 1930, Wayne County reported 1,888,946 residents. Those people had moved off farms or come from elsewhere, but they had no cows. They needed dairy products, and soon the milk peddlers filled the bill.

Milk peddlers were an independent lot. They usually owned one or more cows (in 1900, there were fifteen thousand cows in the city of Detroit), a horse or two and a milk wagon, which was initially an open-air flat wagon. Poorer milk peddlers were licensed as "foot peddlers," and they—or, more commonly, their children—worked the neighborhood. Peddlers would milk their cows in the dark morning and then load the milk cans into their wagons. They then moved up the city streets, selling to customers in tenements or houses on their routes. When a customer—invariably a housewife—needed milk, she would take her pitcher or milk jug to the curb.

The milk peddler ladled milk into her pitcher and collected the cash; standard milk sold for about four to eight cents a quart between the years 1896 and 1915. Part of the problem was that this was raw milk, unrefrigerated but iced down most of the time, sitting in the open air. While milk peddling was common in European cities, it was viewed with intense skepticism in the United States by health officials as the age of food science and interest in food-born illnesses picked up steam. "Deaths from typhoid, intestinal diseases diphtheria, scarlet fever, and pulmonary tuberculosis were frequent when water and food were germ laden," according to former University of Chicago professor Richard Osborn Cummings.

Milk was of prime concern since it carried all the diseases mentioned above and more. A fairly common illness for people in the city or country was then known as "milksick," also called the "slows" or "trembles." Abraham Lincoln's mother died from this in Illinois. A popular explanation was that it resulted from drinking milk of cows that ate white snakeroot weed, but it likely came from milk held in unsanitary conditions. A milk peddler's hands were typically unwashed, ladling raw, unpasteurized milk from open cans on his wagon. The biggest danger was to bottle-

This horse-drawn wagon belonged to Towar Creamery, 1910. *From the papers of the Wolff family (bl004004), Bentley Historical Library, University of Michigan.*

fed infants. Breast-feeding was recommended but not always understood, even by doctors and nurses. Mothers sometimes fed babies condensed milk, which quickly gave infants rickets, as described in the *Detroit Medical Journal* of 1913. When breast milk did not appear immediately after a baby's birth, many mothers and doctors assumed something was wrong. Colustrum, which was exactly what new infants required, looked unusual, so some new mothers decided against breast-feeding. Since there was no Enfamil or Simulac, the alternative was hiring a wet nurse, which produced too much milk too fast for newborns, or bottle-fed milk. The results were devastating: 80 percent of infant deaths in the clinic at Detroit's Children's Free Hospital were from gastrointestinal troubles. It didn't help that many milk peddlers promoted "baby's milk" or "nursery milk" to young mothers; this was usually milk from Jersey cows with higher butter fat or sometimes just plain old regular milk, both harmful to newborns. Mothers who brought infants to hospitals were summarily turned away. There was nothing at the hospital that could save an infant with these problems. It was hopeless.

Along with issues of sanitation, milk peddlers were suspected of "adulterating" milk by adding substances to make it look richer—like chalk or "white earth" gypsum. The following report is from the *Detroit Free Press* in 1879:

STARTLING DISCLOSURES.

A MILK PEDDLER'S INFAMOUS ADULTERATIONS.

Last Monday an indignant citizen brought to police headquarters a considerable quantity of a substance closely resembling, in its damp state, white paint. He informed Supt. Rogers that the substance was the settlings of his days supply of milk, and he had no doubt that his milkman was guilty of adulterating the milk that he peddled.

Other milk peddlers were accused of cheating by watering down the milk, as in this dramatic courtroom encounter captured by the *Free Press* in 1888:

WATERED HIS MILK

August Rahn Pays a fine of $40 in Police Court

August Rahn, a milk peddler, was at the police court yesterday for the second time to answer for a charge of selling watered milk…the milk inspector said the first sample of Rahn's milk showed thirteen percent of water and the last one showed fourteen percent.

"How's this Mr. Rahn?" asked Justice Miner. "You're progressing the wrong way."

"I know nodings vhat he say," replied the milkman.

"He says you are putting water in your milk."

"Vell, everybody knows there is vater in all milk," was the reply.

"Yes," said the court. "But he has a machine in his office that tells when someone puts too much water in."

"I tink he fix it oop. I no trust him. He all time after poor man and let the rich ones go.

FORMALDEHYDE TO KEEP MILK "LOOKING" FRESH

In one notorious scandal that included Towar Creamery, one of Detroit's big milk dealers, formaldehyde was added to milk to preserve its freshness.

In fairness, the dealers and peddlers bought the formaldehyde in bottles from Chicago firms like the Preservaline Manufacturing Company, where it was promoted as a safe additive and sold as "milksweet" or "freezine." Apparently, there was so much freezine in the milk that people could smell it from the pitchers. It didn't enhance peddlers' reputations.

THE MILK INSPECTORS

While most peddlers were honest men, it was up to the city milk inspectors to track down the miscreants. The inspectors were usually police sergeants. At the turn of the century, Detroit had only two milk inspectors to cover milk delivered to 300,000 residents by over 300 peddlers. In 1897, one inspector was Clifton H. Tilden, a Detroit cop who walked the beat in the then rough-and-tumble Irish Corktown. He had a violent temper and chased down peddlers, and frequently their children, who made the deliveries to the door. Another famous inspector was the fearsome Lieutenant Pierce Hanrahan, who "looked like General Sherman" and was a former Indian fighter out West. But those keystone cop types were replaced by a new style of inspector, a medical doctor who knew just how important safe, wholesome milk was in his day. His name was Dr. William H. Price. Price worked with a second inspector, Dr. L. Stuart, running up and down the alleys tracking down peddlers, taking milk samples to the chemist Tibbal's laboratory for testing on the new "lactometer" and inspecting milking parlors, grocers, restaurants or backyard milk sheds, where cows stood in filth with pigs and chickens. Price went after them all as if every baby in Detroit were cheering him on. But it wasn't easy. In 1904, the *Detroit Free Press* reported:

> *DOGS WERE LET LOOSE ON MILK INSPECTOR*
> *When Dr. William H. Price, milk inspector, visited the residence of Frank Karaman on Otis Avenue a day or two ago the family set the dogs on him. Dr. Price, however, proceeded and obtained a view of what was supposed to be a cow's stall. He declared he had never seen so filthy a place. About the time he was well underway…Karaman announced he was going inside after a gun with which to shoot the inspector.*
> *"I didn't stay long after that…"*

Then there was the occasional insane milk peddler, like Joseph Mette, who lived on Harper Avenue and carried a revolver and, as newspapers reported, "has shot at persons who angered him." When not working, Mette "seems to be seized by a curious exaltation and marches up and down his back yard beating a dishpan and singing at the top of his voice. At other times he hurls dishes about the house and smashes furniture."

The Big Players Take Over

At the turn of the century, big national companies began to finance factories to produce canned condensed milk, a process that was begun by entrepreneur Mr. Gail Borden and led to Borden's milk. At the same time, the big Detroit milk dealers united to become even bigger. The Detroit Creamery Company formed in 1897 and by 1916 had built a beautiful state-of-the-art dairy and horse stable at Grand River and Cass Avenue designed by no less an architect than Alfred Kahn.

Milk peddlers began to panic and organized to combat large business concerns from building more processing plants, controlling prices and taking over their routes to drive them out of work. In 1903, the milk peddlers officially formed a union called the Milk Peddlers and Helpers Union. As reported in 1903, "Peddlers who own more than one wagon are ineligible for membership."

Their president was William J. Pickering. They met at Johnson Hall every other Friday, and their first order of business was Sunday deliveries. They delivered milk 365 days a year and wanted a day off. Those peddlers who bought milk from Towar Creamery or Detroit Creamery were told by George H. Towar that he had no objection, but they would need to work all day and night on Saturday, "which they had to admit would not be a satisfactory arrangement."

Over time, the big dealers were prevailing. Detroit Creamery Company had the largest dairy processing plant in the state and was considered by many to be the cleanest plant in the country. Daily, it had 303 wagons, with teams of horses, making a total of fifty thousand stops and selling over twenty thousand gallons of milk. By 1916, it began using motor trucks for wholesale deliveries. Towar Creamery at Grand River and Henry likewise advertised

This building was Detroit Creamery's main plant and depot. It was designed by Albert Kahn. Photo circa 1910. *Author's collection.*

its large, well-ventilated milking parlor called the "Sunshine Plant" due to light that poured in on the cows through tall windows.

In the meantime, Price and his boss, Detroit health officer Dr. Guy L. Kiefer, pressed on with cleaning up the milk supply. Kiefer wrote in 1908 that 65 percent of all Detroit schoolchildren suffered from disease; this was a common statistic in all big American cities. One-third of all high school kids were plagued by hearing or vision problems, and headaches were common. The gloves were off. Improving the city's milk was at top on their list of health issues.

Milk Peddlers Feel the Heat

They passed a series of ordinances; the peddlers fought every one. The first was a license. In 1897, anyone selling milk in Detroit had to have a license displayed on his or her wagon. Foot peddlers wore a badge. The milk peddlers turned up at a Detroit Common Council meeting to intimidate and shout down the proposal, but the council stood firm. Next, Price ordered all milk to be labeled on the milk can, especially skimmed milk. To further reduce airborne germs, milk bottles appeared in the 1880s in New York City and were soon advertised in Detroit. They were improvements over the open-air cans but also caused their own health concerns. For example, milk bottles were being refilled without being washed, let alone scrubbed, boiled and sterilized. Bottles were an expense and a constant irritant to the milk peddlers, who accused housewives of hoarding the bottles for whatever reason. But of course, some Detroiters found an immediate use for milk bottles, as recorded in 1919 in the *Detroit Free Press*: "Milk Bottles This Woman's Best Weapon, Court Is Told. Mrs. Gendelman Let Two Fly through Windows, Former Neighbor Complains; One Hit Baby on Forehead."

Despite the annoyance to milk peddlers, bottles made a significant improvement to health in big cities across the nation. Another ordinance in 1904 required peddlers to ice their milk—no milk over fifty degrees could be sold. The peddlers balked at the price for coolers and ice. The public was beginning to see the need to clean up the backyard dairies in the city. An editorial from the *Detroit Free Press* in 1909 states it clearly:

> *Milk From City Cow Sheds*
> *Popular opinion in Detroit will be very generally on the side the board of health in its culminating effort this week to suppress unsanitary milk barns within the city limits. The impression that the effort is a discrimination against the small dealer who is trying to eke out a livelihood by keeping a few cows is erroneous, as anyone knows who has seen barns in the class complained of by the inspectors…Detroit, like other cities has come to realize that its milk must be pure or it will be dangerous.*

Dr. Price insisted that all milking parlors must have a cement floor with proper drainage and ventilation. This was way beyond the means of most backyard cow dairies, but Price was not through. Land in the city was skyrocketing. More and more milk came from outside Detroit; cities such as Royal Oak, Ann Arbor, Chelsea, Birmingham, Farmington, Northville, Pontiac, Clarenceville, Belleville and Romulus were all providing milk from dairy farms. It was also perceived as healthier than city dairy milk. New York dealt with city "swill milk," which was contaminated milk from cows fed "brewery slops" or "swill" from breweries. Detroit reported instances of swill milk and had several court cases of cows fed garbage or even pickles.

The Milk Outside the City Came by Train

In 1900, the *Detroit Free Press* reported:

> *At different times during the day and night milk wagons from the various farms gather at depots and suburban stations to meet the milk trains… Most of the milk shipped to Detroit arrives at 9 to 12 o'clock at night where it is iced and awaits the milk retailers from 2 to 4:30 in the morning.*

Health officials concluded that this made inspection from farm to home impossible for city officials, even when supported by county and state health organizations. Pasteurization was the only answer, according to Dr. Price, and he wanted every drop of milk in Michigan to be pasteurized. Pasteurization was fairly new in the United States. City papers came out against it at first, but it soon gained acceptance throughout the country. The peddlers were doomed.

Dr. Price was promoted to city health officer in 1913. He hammered hard for pasteurization, and in 1916 Michigan was the first state in the United States to mandate that all milk be pasteurized. By 1921, the health department announced that baby death rates from diarrhea and enteritis in the city of Detroit had dropped by half, from 48.6 to 21.6 per one thousand births attributed to pasteurization and improved milk facilities and supply.

6

Fishing for a Living in Detroit

P eople still cast a rod into the Detroit River today and might pull out a
walleye, muskie or bass. But the fish population is a small fraction of
what it was in the nineteenth century, when fisheries flourished all along
the river and were considered among the most lucrative in the Great Lakes.
Perch, pike, pickerel, sturgeon, lake herring, muskie, walleye and trout—all
were at one time abundant in the Detroit River, and Detroiters went to great
lengths to bring them in.

Detroit ranked second only to Chicago in 1872, handling more than 3.4
million pounds of Great Lakes fresh fish—mostly whitefish and herring.
Much of the fresh fish marketed in Detroit was taken from the spawning
runs of those two species that ascended the river each fall. In 1687, French
explorer Lom d'Arce, Baron de La Hontan, encountered trout "as big as
my thigh." In the Great Lakes, whitefish was by far the most popular catch.

The vast quantities of fish were noticed early in Detroit's history during
British control of the city. The *Commercial Advertiser* reported on December
10, 1824:

> *White-fish, as we have been told by an old inhabitant, were first taken
> with nets in the Detroit River about fifty years ago. It is said that a
> British lieutenant, who was stationed at that time at this post, first
> discovered the movements of the white-fish, and suggested the idea of
> taking them with nets…he had heard at times a rushing noise in the
> water. The lieutenant waited a few minutes, and had the pleasure of*

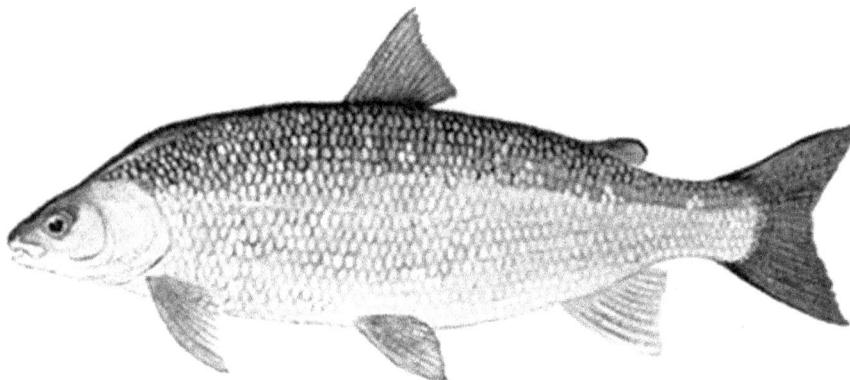

A Great Lakes whitefish.

hearing the rushing, which, as he was somewhat acquainted with fishing, he knew to be caused by an immense number of fish rising to the surface of the water. A small net was immediately got in readiness, and such was the number caught, that, from four dollars, the price soon fell to four shillings a hundred.

FISHING ON BELLE ISLE

Twelve hundred barrels were taken off Belle Isle and sold for five dollars a barrel in 1822. A barrel held 250 cleaned and salted whitefish, so 300,000 fish were harvested. At that time, Belle Isle was called Isle de Couchon (Hog Island) and was privately owned by Monsieur Barnabe Campau, brother of the more famous Joseph Campau, whose name is used for a Detroit Street. Barnabe Campau bought the island from Alexander Macomb. He had worked on the East Coast and saw how they salted codfish and put them in barrels. He decided to try it with

Mackinac boats used for commercial fishing. *National Oceanic and Atmospheric Administration (NOAA).*

Great Lakes freshwater fish and sent ten barrels to Buffalo for ten dollars a barrel. That fish fed workers digging the Erie Canal, and an industry was born. In 1824, on Grosse Ile, 30,000 whitefish were caught from the Detroit River in a single day. Other fisheries were downriver on Grassy Island and another at Ecorse, owned by the Clark brothers.

The whitefish fishing season was in the spring and late fall, mid-October to December. The fish spawned swimming from Lake Erie up the river to Lake St. Clair. Whitefish reach maturity in three to four years, and a fish lays between ten thousand and seventy-five thousand eggs in its lifetime, depending on its size. Whitefish were bigger then, typically reaching ten pounds and sometimes fifteen pounds. In the 1860s, they were sold for a nickel a dozen at the Central Market in Detroit, but if you cared to venture to one of the fisheries where they were hauled in with nets, you could take all you wanted for free.

The fish was so highly thought of by nineteenth-century Indian agent, naturalist and writer Henry Schoolcraft that he wrote a poem to the whitefish:

All friends of good living by tureen and dish
Concur in exalting this prince of a fish,
So fine in a platter, so tempting a fry,
So rich on a gridiron, so sweet in a pie,
That even before it the salmon must fail,
And that mighty bonne-bouce the land beaver's tail.

Its beauty and flavor no person can doubt,
When seen in the water or tasted without.
And all the dispute that opinion ere makes
Of this king of lake-fishes, this deer of the lake,
Regards not its choiceness to ponder or sup
But its best mode of dressing and serving it up.

The earliest commercial fishing was "seine" or large-net fishing. On the Detroit River, families of French Detroiters and Canadians, brothers and cousins, fished together. From 1819 to 1879, everyone fishing on Belle Isle had the same name: Campau. Some crews had three generations of family who worked side by side. They were divided into crews, so someone was fishing while the other crew rested.

The large seine was 30 feet wide and 36 fathoms (216 feet) long. It had a bottom line weighted with lead, which would sink it, and a top line of cork or cedar floats painted red and spaced out every 25 feet. Empty kegs were used here and there to add buoyancy to two 1,200-foot ropes attached to the seine.

The seine was piled into a giant canoe manned by three young men wearing oilskins, boots and heavy jersey coats. The crew launched the canoe from a small platform at night, paddling to a buoy marker in the river. These were tough men to endure the choppy, icy November river, the bitter wind and rain or snow at night; many were former fur trappers or Canadian voyagers who took up fishing as the fur industry faded.

As two men paddled heading north from the Canadian side of Belle Isle, one man stood at the "table" that held the net in the boat's stern and carefully paid out the seine, making sure it didn't tangle. On Belle Isle, the ropes tied to the seine were threaded through two posts—a ten-foot-high post called a "land brail" and a second, higher "sea brail," which kept them apart. When the boat crew reached the line's end, they'd signal to the shore. Then, in a small shed on the platform, two horses were made ready. One would begin a slow circular walk to turn the capstan, a winch, and reel in one end of the rope tied to the seine. The net would balloon out like a giant bag. After some time, the second horse would begin gradually bringing the open net together and back to shore. After paddling for more than a mile, the boat crew would return and, with others on the shore, begin hauling in the net and "the hundreds of wriggling, shimmering fish of many kinds and sizes," as reported in the newspaper. In good seasons, the fish ran as high as one thousand to a net, and they ran incessantly for ten days around the clear waters of Belle Isle's "North Point." In the month of July 1857, at one haul, 45,700 whitefish were brought to the beach, and for nine consecutive days, the smallest haul was 18,000 fish.

The fisheries were operated on a cooperative basis, as were many family businesses. The first 10,000 fish paid expenses; after that, the owner took half the catch, and the crew split the other half. Each crew member was also given 250 fish for his own use. They were a colorful lot, sitting beside their bunkhouse shanties in the autumn evenings, smoking clay pipes and watching the farmers across the river on the Canadian shore harvest crops. A campfire was always kept burning on the beach.

Detroiters talked nostalgically about hearing the fishermen sing their old chansons on the boats as they paddled and worked the nets to the song's rhythm:

> *Dans le prison de Nantes,*
> *Il y a un prisonnier*
> *Il y a un prisonnier*
> *Que personne ne va vois,*
> *Que la fille du geôlier.*

> *In the prison of Nantes*
> *There is a prisoner*
> *There is a prisoner*
> *Whom nobody goes to see*
> *But the daughter of the jailer.*

Some fisheries, such as Clark's near Ecorse, built giant holding pens using planks and nets in the river. They would dump their catch into the holding pens to keep live whitefish or lake herring to sell at the ready when needed throughout the year.

POUND NETS

During the middle of the nineteenth century, a new innovation arrived from Connecticut with emigrants from New England. It was called the pound net or trap net and was originally used on the Connecticut River. It was a long net system staked into the lake bed that lured fish into the "lead"—a tunnel that guided the fish to the circular "pound" and then opened to the square "pot," which held the fish securely until the fishermen could pull the fish out.

The biggest difference between pound nets versus seine fishing was that seine fishing was done from land, and to do it you had to own the land, such as the Campau's Fishery on Belle Isle. Pound netters set up the nets and fished from boats. At the start, their fishing boats were called "pound net boats" and were small, flat-bottomed, single-mast sailboats or, in some cases, rowboats.

Later, steam-powered boats were used. Soon, there were hundreds of men and women in the commercial fishing business. Lake Erie was the most popular spot for pound nets since the lake was relatively shallow and the bottom sandy clay, which was soft enough to drive in the stakes but firm enough to keep them stable.

Pound nets required stakes to hold the nets—initially, iron-hard white oak tree saplings pounded into the lake bottom from three to ten feet. Western Lake Erie had hundreds of pound nets during the fall and spring fishing season. In 1885, there were 888 pound nets on the southern side of Lake Erie from Detroit to Cleveland. This soon became a more capital-intensive form of fishing, requiring a boat, nets and a device to pound in the stakes and another to remove the stakes.

Fishing with pound nets grew too costly for small-time fisheries and was dominated by "dealers," who owned multiple sites and hired fishermen to tend the nets. At the height of the season, small crews of fishermen tended the nets daily, going out at daybreak. They would empty the pot by lifting the front of it (the crib) to crowd the fish together, a process called "shoaling up." The fish were then scooped out. The work was very strenuous.

Emptying pound nets on Lake Erie. *National Oceanic and Atmospheric Administration (NOAA).*

By the second half of the nineteenth century, as boats got larger, fisheries used steam-driven pile drivers to hammer the stakes into the lake bottom. In Lake Erie, the nets stretched for ten miles into the water from shore, while in Lake Michigan and Lake Superior the lashed stakes could be ninety-seven feet deep.

Pound netters were supposed to remove the nets and stakes at the end of the season, in the fall and spring. That didn't always happen. Sometimes the stakes would break off as the fishermen tried to pull them out, leaving a jagged spike just below the surface of the water. These nets became a serious menace to ships trying to steam from Detroit east to Sandusky. Lake Erie became a gauntlet of netting and posts, some of which were fifty feet long and ten inches in diameter at the butt and seven inches at the top, according to a report from the U.S. Commission of Fish and Fisheries of 1897.

As one shipowner in 1893 said in a letter to the editor of the *Detroit Free Press*:

> *I know it to be a fact that good, substantial vessels have had good-sized holes punched in their bottoms from no other cause. Besides this it is an*

Washing pound nets. *National Oceanic and Atmospheric Administration (NOAA).*

impossibility for any vessel to steer a course through this tangle. A ship going from Detroit to Toledo or Sandusky would have to steer a zig-zag course that would be miles more than necessary.

If there was fog on the river or lake, vessels sometimes became entirely entangled in nets and poles and had to be abandoned. For sailing ships, it became so difficult that they had to be towed through the maze. On the other hand, pound net dealers regularly complained that their nets were run over and destroyed by vindictive shipowners.

GILL NETS

Gill nets are very old, used by Ottawa fishermen on the Great Lakes well before the Europeans arrived. Gill net fishing changed in the latter 1800s with the emergence of the "fishing steamer." The early

A gill net on a reel to dry. *National Oceanic and Atmospheric Administration (NOAA).*

commercial gill netters used sailboats or rowboats and stayed close to shore, unable to handle big storms on the lakes. The fishing steamer was actually a tugboat that would tow the rowboats out to deeper water and then, at the end of the day, tow them back to shore. It did not take long before gill nets were put directly on the tugs. This allowed gill nets to go thirty miles away from shore to catch fish in the deep water. They could also cruise up Lake Erie and the Detroit River to follow spawning schools of fish, a technique that was very destructive to fish populations. Canadians referred to it at the time as "American fishing."

Commercial gill net fishing was controversial from the start. Pound netters and gill netters argued back and forth about who was destroying commercial fishing faster. Gill nets were more wasteful than other forms of commercial fishing; fish were trapped by their gills in the netting. When the nets were pulled up, the fish were dead. However, if a net went untended for too long, within a few days the fish would decay and were not marketable so were thrown out. There was much argument that the mesh size of the gill nets was too small.

A small mesh caught all species of fish, especially underweight fish. During storms, nets broke loose and were set afloat with entrapped fish. In Lake Michigan, as many as three thousand nets were lost in the autumn of 1879, carrying down 500,000 to 600,000 whitefish. Such massive numbers of decaying fish destroyed spawning grounds. As Margaret Beattie Bogue reported in her book *Fishing the Great Lakes* in 1885, the estimate of lost fish due to rotting in gill nets was four to five hundred tons in Lake Erie alone. Gill nets had become the dominant commercial method of fishing in the Detroit River by the latter half of the nineteenth century since the current and depth of the river made pound nets difficult to use.

A gill net sailing vessel carried sixty to one hundred nets into the Great Lakes, according to the Commission of Fish and Fisheries Report of 1885. Nets were from two to three hundred feet long but could run as long as six hundred feet. In 1885, it was recorded that fishermen on the Great Lakes used ninety-seven thousand gill nets extending 5,300 miles in total length.

Pound netters worked hard but lived and worked close to home. Gill netters' lives were more difficult and dangerous. They could be gone for long periods. On the west side of the state, close to 90 percent of the gill net crews working Lake Michigan were Dutch. The lives of these men were hard. They fished twenty to thirty miles from shore. As reported by a fish hatcheries superintendent in the 1890s:

> *The lives of the lake fishermen are not easy ones. In all kinds of weather the nets must be looked after and usually the catch is largest when the great gales sweep the lakes…Oil skins sheeted with ice, numb fingers cut and bleeding from drawing in freezing nets, and faces frost bitten by icy spray are common experiences.*

Lifting three-hundred-foot gill nets filled with fish was extremely difficult, dangerous labor and was done by hand until 1890, when steam-powered lifters arrived. Over the years, nets got bigger. A pound net of an enormous size was used at Wellington Beach on Lake Ontario, one having a perimeter of 3,363 feet and a depth of about 29 feet, covering an area of four acres.

As early as the 1860s, newspapers reported that catches were getting smaller, and it was growing obvious that the fish were disappearing. They were being fished out. The son of Barnabe Campau, Alexander Campau, tried with others to limit the catches and numbers of fisheries, but their efforts were too late.

In addition, in the 1860s, sawdust from the logging mills, such as Nelson and Company in Muskegon, was being dumped on the beaches, destroying whitefish breeding grounds. Pollution from industry, such as the residue of burned coal (clinkers) from growing iron foundries, was being dumped in the river, killing fish.

FISHING GETS NASTY

Over the years, fishermen could be a quarrelsome lot. They sued one another in court or passed state laws to control one another, but as the fish began to grow scarce, things got more serious.

Fisheries in the Detroit River accused the pound netters in Lake Erie of wiping out the spawning season. In 1894, Canadians brought in the Lake Huron cruiser the *Petrel* to tear out hundreds of gill nets on the Canadian side of Lake Erie. The British captain of the *Petrel* stated, "The persistence of the American fishermen is due to the fact that all the good fishing grounds on the American side are literally filled with nets."

Gill nets were forbidden on Ohio's side of Lake Erie, and when the Michigan fishermen refused to leave their fishing beds, the fish commissioner used a tugboat and a shotgun to chase them out. Debate began in the Michigan legislature on a "closed season" for whitefish to forbid fishing during the fall breeding season to allow the fish to recover. Fishermen favored this, but the powerful pound net fish dealers fought against any interruption of supply; they favored a system of state hatcheries to replenish the fish. The state had hatcheries in Northville, took over the Belle Isle fisheries and started the Willis Hatchery.

From a catch of about four thousand fish in 1907, they could produce more than 100 million eggs. But the water conditions continued to deteriorate due to industrial pollution. In 1913, the Detroit River was dredged to improve shipping, destroying whitefish spawning grounds. Soon, the fish, fisheries and fishermen were gone. In less than a lifetime, the Great Lakes were depleted to the point where commercial fishing was no longer viable.

On a positive note, scientists from the U.S. Geological Survey and U.S. Fish and Wildlife Service discovered spawning lake whitefish and fertilized

Workers collecting eggs from whitefish at the Northville Fishery. *Courtesy of the Northville Historical Society.*

whitefish eggs in the Detroit River in the fall of 2006, the first documented spawning of the fish in the river since 1916. As they claim, "The discovery provides further evidence of progress in the ecological recovery of the Detroit River."

7

Passenger Pigeons' Last Stand

William Butts Mershon lived his life in Saginaw. He was born in 1856, and in the 1870s, as a teen, he loved to hunt. His father, who owned a planing lumber mill in Saginaw, went hunting with him; while his mother didn't hunt, she made the lunch basket and occasionally went with them into the woods. She would hold the horse while they hunted birds like grouse or partridge. Because the black powder used with the old fowling pieces created so much smoke when fired, she would call out to tell them if they hit their mark. And Mershon said that his mother loved and looked after their bird dogs: Sport, Bob and Ranger.

He wrote much later as an adult:

> *You may be curious to know what I look like as we trudge along Indian file…I am a chunk of a country lad topped by a woolen cap with ear tabs pulled down over my ears, a tippet* [a long dangling scarf] *around my neck, yarn mittens on my hands…my everyday pants are tucked into calfskin boots. My Irish water spaniel "Sport" is tagging along behind. My gun is a sixteen gauge muzzle loader, sub and twist barrels, with dogs heads for hammers.*

Mershon's favorite game birds were passenger pigeons. He would wait for the first sign of their return in April:

PASSENGER PIGEON (*Columba Migratoria*)

A John James Audubon print of the passenger pigeon, 1824.

Outdoorsman William B. Mershon of Saginaw, seen here in the 1870s, wrote a book on passenger pigeons in 1907, less than a decade after the last wild pigeons had been killed. *Local History & Genealogy Collection, Public Libraries of Saginaw.*

There was a flight of pigeons that morning, the first one of the season and behind the foremost flock another and another came streaming…they swept like a cloud. Crossing the river to the west they reached the woods near Jerome's mill and skirted the clearings or passed in waves over the tree tops, back of John Winter's farm, and then wheeled to the south.

Once in range, he took little time to shoot and bring home birds by the dozens. As he said, "I was reckoned a pretty good shot and have a first rate gun." The only blemish on his hunting experiences was what he called "poachers." These were "the low-down men who would steal my birds." They would shoot beside him and then dash over and grab up all his birds and walk away. Since he was a boy, there was little he could do about them, and his hatred of these thieves would only increase as he grew up.

Passenger pigeons—or, as they were called in Mershon's days, "wild pigeons"—were the most common wild fowl found in the Detroit farmers' markets throughout the nineteenth century. They were similar in appearance

Simon Pokagon of St. Joseph, Michigan, was a Pottawatomie chief, author and respected naturalist. *From Chief Pokagon's book* Queen of the Woods, *1899.*

to mourning doves but larger, with a slender neck, long tail feathers and narrow wings. They were more colorful than mourning doves, with a dark blue head, back and shoulders, a golden-hued neck and a rusty breast that faded to white at the belly.

Of course, they were well known in Michigan to the native Indians. During his day, Pottawatomie chief Simon Pokagon from St. Joseph, Michigan, was a nationally known nature writer for magazines like *Forest and Stream*. He wrote that the birds were called *O-me-me-wog*: "It was proverbial with our fathers that if the Great Spirit had made a more elegant bird in plumage, form, and movement, He never did."

The birds moved across the Great Lakes and the Midwest to the north as far as Hudson's Bay and to Louisiana forests in staggering millions upon millions, in deafening and defecating flocks roaring over the forests, farms and lakes. Michigan was an important source of food and roost (some birds roost as a group at night for protection against natural predators), with large nesting areas near Petoskey, Traverse City, Ludington, St. Joseph and elsewhere throughout the state. The Pigeon River Area of northern

Michigan was so named because of the birds. And their last great roost in 1879 was near Petoskey. It has been estimated that at one time one out of three wild birds in America was a passenger pigeon; between three to five billion of them flew in endless undulating flocks through the skies. Chief Pokagon wrote in 1895 for another outdoor magazine, *Chautuaguan*:

When a young man I have stood for hours admiring the movements of these birds…ever varying in hue; and as the mighty stream, sweeping on at sixty miles an hour, reached some deep valley, it would pour its living mass headlong down hundreds of feet, sounding as though a whirlwind was abroad in the land…The sound of the birds was a mingling of sleigh bells, mixed with the rumbling of an approaching storm. While I gazed in wonder and astonishment, I beheld moving toward me in an unbroken front millions of pigeons…they passed like a cloud through the branches of the high trees, through the underbrush and over the ground apparently overturning every leaf. Statue-like I stood half concealed by cedar boughs. They fluttered all about me, lighting on my head and shoulders; gently I caught two in my hands and carefully concealed them under my blanket.

They were called passenger pigeons because they flew in a mass like passengers from one spot to another. They did not migrate as other birds do from one locale to another as the seasons change but moved from roost to roost feasting on the "mast"—or seeds, pine seeds, acorns, hack berries, hempseed, huckleberries, beech nuts, hemlock seeds, worms, caterpillars, Indian corn, rye and wheat—in the trees, bushes and forest floor and hastening their demise.

The famous ornithologist Alexander Wilson estimated that the pigeons he dissected averaged a half pint of mast in their gullets. One flock he observed that was 1 mile wide and 240 miles long consumed over 17,424,000 million bushels of "the fruits of the forest" a day. The flocks excoriated the landscape not only of food but also of trees. The sheer mass of so many birds collapsed trees. Hundreds nested in single trees. Alexander Wilson described the destruction caused by the enormous flocks as they roosted:

The ground is covered to the depth of several inches with their dung; all the tender grass and under wood destroyed; the surface strewed with large limbs of trees broken down by the weight of the birds clustering one above another; and the trees themselves, for thousands of acres, killed as completely as if girdled by an ax.

A fog or snowstorm over the lake produced thousands of dead birds. One merchant captain on Lake Huron recorded masses of dead birds in the water for three hours as he chugged along the coast. A fog had confused them.

The farmers had no love for the pigeons. The *Niles Republican* reported in May 1860:

> The wild pigeons in various localities have been very destructive to corn…We hear of farmers who have had from 10 to 20 acres pulled out. Their nesting places are in the woods near the shoreline from which they pour forth in the morning by the thousands in search of food.

Another report from the *Detroit Free Press* in 1858 stated:

> Wild pigeons sweep the late planted cornfields clean, pulling up the stalks and devouring every grain…They cannot be driven away for when fired at they only rise to light again within a few rods.

Sullivan Cook wrote for *Forest and Stream* magazine in 1903:

> When a boy…I often had to go with a gun and drive the pigeons from the newly sown fields of wheat. Pigeons would come by the thousands and pick up the wheat before it could be covered with the drag. My father would say, "Get the gun and shoot every pigeon you see," and I would see them…alighting on the newly sown field. They would alight until the ground was fairly blue with these beautiful birds.

The Commercial Market Emerges

Early on, there was little need for pigeons beyond personal use. People cooked them into pigeon pie in Detroit. This was la tourtière—a meat pie made with pigeons. They pickled pigeon breasts in vinegar to preserve them. They broiled them, roasted them, fricaseed them and made them into soup. Farmers fed dead pigeons to pigs. They made a form of duck confit called "jugged pigeon."

But soon, there began to be a commercial market for passenger pigeon in the cities. At first, some farmers would simply take their pigeons to town

A passenger pigeon shoot.

and sell them for ten cents a dozen. But others began using dealers to ship dressed pigeons. In Chicago, they sold for fifty to sixty cents a dozen. Baby pigeons, called "squabs," fetched even more. Pigeons were shipped to the southern United States to feed slaves. There was a burgeoning market for live pigeons to be used in shooting contests. But the big market was New York City and Boston, where pigeons fetched two dollars a dozen by the late 1870s. The ornithologist John James Audubon recorded schooners in the Hudson River that he assumed were piled with coal but after a closer look saw were heaped with mountains of dead passenger pigeons dressed and waiting to be sold to New York markets and restaurants. Michigan was a major source for pigeons sold to New York and New England markets since the eastern United States had been hunted out.

In Detroit, the biggest wild game dealer was H.T. Phillips. He was known throughout the United States and even in Europe for wild game. Mr. Phillips

A variety of game birds hang from the side of William B. Mershon's hunting train car, the City of Saginaw. Besides hunters, professional "pigeoners" and farmers shot or trapped the birds for sale in eastern markets. *Local History & Genealogy Collection Public Libraries of Saginaw.*

supplied hotels with bear meat, he was the largest dealer of wild venison in the country and he was the biggest dealer of pigeons in Michigan. Ironically, he was an active member of the Audubon Society and was an expert shot, and unlike other dealers, he bought pigeons only in season. He tried to get the small Michigan towns to stop sending so many pigeons and at times refused to buy them.

In Detroit during "pigeon season," it was said you could kill hundreds of birds by swinging a walking stick at them. Thomas DeVoe relates in his book *Market Assistant* that a man in Detroit was reported by the *Owosso News* to hold the record of catching birds in the single swoosh of his long-handled net, which were commonly used to catch and kill the birds: "Mr. Merritt on Wednesday last, caught, at one haul of his net, six hundred and forty-eight wild pigeons."

Single birds were rigged to a stool and made to move about, attracting hundreds of birds to be captured. (It is how we got the term "stool pigeon.") The opening of railroads linking the Great Lakes area with New York meant that 300,000 passenger pigeons were sent to New York in 1855. However, the most devastating killings were during the 1860s and 1870s. The figures were recorded as a normal part of commerce by the H.T. Phillips Company:

> *1860 (23 July) saw 235,200 birds sent east from Grand Rapids;*
> *In 1869, Van Buren County, Michigan, shipped 7,500,000 birds to the east.*
> *1874 saw 1,000,000 birds shipped east from Oceana County;*
> *1876 saw 1,600,000 shipped east from Oceana County (400,000 per week during the season).*
> *In 1880, 527,000 birds were shipped east from Michigan.*

Audubon writes in his autobiography about his experience with passenger pigeons in Ohio:

> *I arrived there nearly two hours before sunset. Few pigeons were to be seen, but a great number of persons with horses and wagons, guns and ammunition, had already established encampments on the borders. Two farmers from the vicinity of Russelville, distant more than one hundred miles, had driven upward of three hundred hogs to be fattened on the pigeons which were to be slaughtered...The dung lay several inches deep, covering the whole extent of the roosting place like a bed of snow. Many trees two feet in diameter, I observed were broken off at no great distance from the ground and the branches of many of the largest and tallest had given way as if the forest had been swept by a tornado. Everything proved to me the number of birds...must be immense beyond conception. As the period of their arrival approached, their foes anxiously prepared to receive them. Some were furnished with iron pots containing sulfur (to burn and asphyxiate them) others with torches of pine knots, many with poles, and the rest with guns. Everything was ready, and all eyes were gazing on the clear sky which appeared in glimpses amidst the tall trees. Suddenly there burst forth a general cry of "Here they come!" The noise which they made, though yet distant, reminded me of a hard gale at sea passing through the rigging...As the birds arrived and passed over me, I felt a current of air that surprised me. Thousands were soon knocked down by the pole men. The birds continued to pour in. The fires were lighted and a magnificent as well as wonderful and almost terrifying sight presented itself. The pigeons, arriving by the thousands, alighted everywhere, one above another until solid masses as large as hogsheads* [as in wine hogsheads, barrel sized] *were formed on the branches*

all around. Here and there perches gave way under the weight with a crash, and, falling to the ground, destroyed hundreds of birds beneath, forcing down the dense groups with which every stick was loaded. It was a scene of uproar and confusion. I found it quite useless to speak, or even to shout to those persons who were nearest to me. Even the reports of the guns were seldom heard, and I was made aware of the firing only by seeing the shooters reloading.

PETOSKEY: THE PIGEONS' FINAL STAND

Heavenly Father, bless us,
And keep us all alive.
There's ten of us to dinner
And not enough for five.
—*Anonymous, "Hodge's Grace," 1850*

The pigeon kill in 1879 outside Petoskey, Michigan, was considered the last big slaughter of pigeons, leading to their extinction. By the 1860s and '70s, there was a group of five hundred men who called themselves professional "pigeoners." Their killing methods, the railroad and the advent of the telegraph, which kept them aware at all times of the flocks, ensured the pigeons' doom. However, most people who killed pigeons were farmers and their families.

H.T. Phillips wrote to Mershon regularly after he retired in 1904, reminiscing about the pigeon business. As he said in one letter, "There were six hundred names in my register book of pigeoners…Nearly everyone of the farmers, and their wives and daughters were pigeon catchers."

During these times, farming in and around Petoskey was brutal for the pioneer homesteaders. After purchasing the forty or eighty acres of northern land from the land grant office in Detroit with little money, they walked sometimes from Detroit to get there, toting their belongings on their backs. Once they reached the Petoskey area, there were few roads, so they walked through deep forest to find their forty or eighty acres. Many of them were veterans of the Civil War. Some of them were men who had lost their shirts in the Panic of '73 (also known as the "Long Depression," which lasted until 1876) and needed a new start.

Professional "pigeoners" with their equipment in Michigan.

Few of these settlers were woodsmen or experienced farmers, and many had only enough money to get to Petoskey, assured that they could sell the trees on their acreage for capital to get started. In most cases, the trees were left untouched or were chopped and burned, for there was at that time no profitable way to haul them through the woods and get them out to market. It was more important to get a place cleared for a potato patch than to worry about selling trees.

In Petoskey and northern Michigan, they were called "mossbacks." These were the men and their families who lived in holes dug in the ground until they could get cabins up. They worked till they dropped from exposure and exhaustion. Then, in the spring of 1877, after an extended winter, fearful tales started coming out of Petoskey. The mossbacks were starving. From the view of the starving settlers, the arrival of the pigeons was nothing less than a miracle, a gift from God.

By this time, William B. Mershon was already a wealthy man. He'd made a fortune in the lumber business. With his brother, he started a successful band saw business and had several other ventures. Later, he was the mayor of Saginaw from 1895 to 1896. He was an avid outdoorsman and had a train car he called the City of Saginaw equipped for hunting parties across Michigan and the western United States. His friends called him Billy or Captain Bill on the train car. President Grover Cleveland was invited on the car. Mershon was a gourmet cook, had a respected wine cellar and read and wrote poetry along with superbly written essays on fishing, hunting and the outdoor life. He was on the board of every outdoor association or club in Saginaw and Michigan, founding most of them. But like many hunters and outdoor sportsmen, the relentless slaughter of wildlife—such as passenger pigeons—infuriated him and left him sickened; for Mershon, it was likely that the professional pigeoners were no different than the poachers who stole his kill as a boy.

The coming pigeon kill in Petoskey was well known. Mershon equipped his train car and sent four friends to Petoskey to witness lawbreaking; there were laws protecting pigeons, but they were weak, unenforceable and completely ignored.

The pigeoners poured into Petoskey. They were everywhere: the hotels, the post office and the streets. Mershon's friend noted from the hotel register that they came from New York, Wisconsin, Pennsylvania, Michigan, Maryland, Iowa, Virginia, Ohio, Texas, Illinois, Maine, Minnesota and Missouri. The pigeoners hurried about town comparing market reports, discussing the price for squabs and quotes for live birds. They established packinghouses and wagons with teams for hauling out dead birds. Locals would be hired for these jobs, as well as being trained on trapping and killing birds.

The pigeons arrived by the millions to roost, and the pigeoners were stretched out alongside the birds for forty miles. They killed birds from daylight to dark, hauling wagon after wagon of dead and live birds for fifty days without cease. It was estimated that they may have killed one billion birds.

Mershon's men rode horses up and down the line, breaking traps, harassing the pigeoners and prodding the lone overworked sheriff to prevent illegal slaughter. The men were seen as a nuisance and chased off with shotguns. Eventually, by summer, it was over. They wrote about their efforts "to check the slaughter" in a Chicago magazine, *American Field Magazine.* A music professor and friend of Mershon's, H.B. Roney, who led the group, said that the work was futile: four against two thousand (professionals and locals).

To counter the bad publicity, one Chicago game dealer, E.T. Martin, to whom Mershon later referred as the "pigeon butcher" in his book, issued a pamphlet in which he justified the killing of pigeons in Petoskey:

Martha, the last passenger pigeon
in captivity, died in 1914.

*This whole pigeon trade was a perfect Godsend to a large portion of
Emmett County. The land outside of Petoskey is taken up by homesteaders,
who, between clearing their land, scanty crops, poor soil, large families, and
small capital are poorer than Job's turkey's prodigal son...and in years past
have had all they could do fighting famine and cold...harrowing tales of
need and destitution.*

Mershon spent the rest of his life trying to find remnants of the great
flocks of passenger pigeons, hoping they were not extinct but merely
scattered or relocated. He wrote to people across the country; he exchanged
letters with John Burroughs, the famous California naturalist who reported
seeing passenger pigeons in Texas and New York in 1906. Chief Pokagon
reported a small flock of nesting pigeons at the headwaters of the Au Sable
River. Mershon would take his rail car out to confirm sightings, but he could
never find the pigeons. The reports were either mistaken about the birds
(flocks of curlews were confused for passenger pigeons), or they were faked
by hunting guides.

Contemporary biological studies of the birds show that they were highly gregarious and required huge numbers to court and nest. A captive pigeon believed to be the world's last passenger pigeon, named Martha, died on September 1, 1914, in Cincinnati.

W.B. Mershon died in Saginaw in 1943 after years of a long illness, his pigeons "that swept like a cloud across the sky" long gone. In his quiet days alone, the lines of the poem "In Evening Air" by the great Saginaw poet Theodore Roethke might have been something he would understand:

> *I see, in evening air,*
> *how slowly dark comes down on what we do.*

PART III
COOKING AT HOME

8

From Stone Hearth
to Cookstove

U p until the Civil War, most Detroiters and Americans still cooked on an open hearth or fireplace, even in tenement buildings and city apartments. This was the case until well after the Civil War for some families. The hearth was the home's center. Though there is no etymological connection, "hearth" sounds like "heart," and for some it was just that—the heart of the home. It was warmth and security and held delicious smells wafting from endlessly simmering iron cooking kettles. In the evening, people read by the hearth, chatted, played cards, spun wool, smoked pipes, darned socks and drifted to sleep. And when the hearth went cold, the house became very dark.

One popular syndicated newspaper column that originated in Ohio and ran for nearly fifteen years in the mid-nineteenth century was called "Farm and Fireplace," and those two places were the world for many Americans. The guardian and keeper of the hearth was the mother, the personification of a contented home. Many considered the hearth a spiritual place. Some hearths in eighteenth-century New England were so large that they were built with a low brick shelf along the inside wall. When dinner was done and the fire had subsided to warm coals, children were allowed to sit on those shelves, chat sweetly and stare up the chimney at the twinkling stars above.

But cooking breakfast and dinner (there was no such thing as lunch) was not so romantic for women. First, the fireplace cooked the cooker about as much as it cooked food. It was dangerous. Cooking tools were basically iron

In 1885, Thomas Palmer gave his wife a present: a rustic log cabin, just like they used to see in the old days, built to her specifications, suitable for summering and entertaining. It was completed in 1887. This photo shows the dining room. *U.S. Library of Congress.*

"cranes" hinged to the side walls that could hang pots, hooks and various crude implements like "toasters." Heat was regulated by swinging the crane and the pot on or off the fire or using a "trammel," a saw-toothed iron piece that allowed the cook to adjust the height of pots above the fire.

Henry Ormal Severence wrote about Michigan settlers' experiences at the hearth in the early 1800s in a wonderful book called *Michigan Trailblazers.* A girl of twelve, Louisa, had to take over the house when her mother died, reminiscing in her old age:

> *The glamour of my tasks vanished in a few weeks. The hard work of lifting the heavy kettles and hanging them on the crane, preparing potatoes*

and cooking bread in the bake oven and getting meals on the table for our family of six was more than I could stand up under.

Iron cooking utensils that needed to be cleaned, such as meat "spits," were excoriated with sand mixed with water. Some iron kettles were fixed with three short iron legs to keep them above the coals. And a cast-iron grate called a gridiron was used for grilling chops, birds, fish and steaks. Steaks were loved then, as now, such as the following recipe of Eliza Leslie's from 1837. Ms. Leslie was a cookbook author well known during her day across the United States, including Detroit. This is a hearth-grilled steak (it was referred to as "broiling" in Ms. Leslie's day) from her cookbook *Directions for Cookery in Its Various Branches*. It would be respected in any steakhouse today:

To Broil Beef Steaks
The best beef-steaks are those cut from the ribs or from the inside of the sirloin. They should be cut about three quarters of an inch thick…Have ready on your hearth a fine bed of clear bright coals, entirely free from smoke and ashes. Set the gridiron over the coals in a slanting direction, that the meat may not be smoked by the fat dropping into the fire directly under it. When the gridiron is quite hot, rub the bars with suet, sprinkle a little salt over the coals, and lay on the steaks. Turn them frequently with a pair of steak-tongs, or with a knife and fork…For those who like them underdone or rare, ten or twelve minutes will be enough…After they are browned, cover the upper side of the steaks with an inverted plate or dish to prevent the flavor from evaporating. Rub a dish with a shallot, or small onion, and place it near the gridiron and close to the fire, that it may be well heated. When the steaks are done, sprinkle them with a little salt and pepper, and lay them in a hot dish, putting on each a piece of fresh butter. Send the steaks to table very hot, in a covered dish. You may serve up with them onion sauce in a small tureen. Pickles are frequently eaten with beef-steaks.

Few home cooks used measuring methods for daily cooking, so ingredients were roughly guessed—a pinch, a dab, a teacup of sugar, a wineglass of brandy or an "addition of butter the size of a hen's egg" were typical. Cooking on a hearth also made temperature control imprecise or nearly impossible, whether on a hearth or a coal-burning stove. One New England cookbook by Ester Allen Howland from 1845 gives instructions on maintaining the proper cooking fire:

A traditional pioneer hearth. *U.S. Library of Congress.*

> *The degree of heat most desirable for dressing the different sorts of food ought to be attended to with the utmost precision…For pies, cakes, and white bread, the heat should be such, that you can hold your hand and arm in while you count forty: for brown bread, meats, beans, Indian puddings, and pumpkin pies, it should be hotter, so that you can only hold it in while you count twenty.*

Forty years later, in 1884, not much improvement was seen on a coal-burning range-top stove in Detroit, as reported in the *Detroit Free Press*:

> *I can't hire a cook who can bake a loaf of bread properly, much less a cake. The moment my back is turned the cook becomes obsessed with insane freak to fill the stove with coal. Then she sits down and forgets it. She burns up whatever I leave in the oven.*

On top of that, cooking on a hearth was exhausting, smoky and dangerous to women and small children. Keeping the hearth cleaned was a full-time effort, as instructed in the *Good Housekeeper,* a bestselling book of home economics from 1839:

> *Keep your kitchen, and all the utensils clean and neat as possible. Sweep the chimney often, with an old broom kept for the purpose, so that no soot may collect to fall down on the dishes at the fire, and be sure that the hearth is neat as a table.*

However, the larger problem with hearths was their cost and inefficiency; they burned ten times the amount of wood as a wood-burning stove. The *Good Housekeeper* discusses the problem:

> *All the culinary processes were carried on with one immense open grate, burning as much fuel in one day as might do the same work for ten. The cook and the furniture of the kitchen get a proportion of this heat, the articles to be dressed another portion, but by far the greatest quantity goes up the chimney.*

If you lived on land with trees, most likely your men folk and the workhorse spent winters hauling sledges loaded with cordwood for the hearth. If you did not, fuel became an issue. As the cities expanded, more trees were cleared while more people arrived. This meant the cordwood had to be carted farther and farther from woods to market, adding to the expense. For example, in Detroit by 1840, cordwood that had for decades been taken from surrounding forests now had to be shipped in by boat from northern Michigan and Canada. Transporting the cordwood was becoming more costly than the wood itself. It was at that moment that the cookstove arrived.

THE STOVE

Stoves were invented in the eighteenth century in Germany. As the nineteenth century began, few stoves for either cooking or heating were found in American homes. The earliest stoves were actually large, crude, blocky cast-iron furnaces. They were sold to the elite; Thomas Jefferson had one of the first stoves installed.

Initially, they were designed and sold as heating stoves, like space heaters, for large rooms like hospitals and hotels. Later stoves were adapted for homes, and soon thereafter, flat tops were added for cooking. Then, as the market demand began to emerge, technical and design improvements also began to develop. The casting of the iron sides of the stove had been completed at small country foundries, unchanged since the Revolutionary War. Iron ore was melted in crude blast furnaces. The molten iron was poured down troughs into forms made from sand or dirt on the ground in the middle of open fields. The result was ragged, rough, uneven castings with pits and cracks, little control of the process and no design. The U.S. stove manufacturers moved the casting indoors and began using carved oak panels as molds, as explained by Howell John Harris in his excellent research on the stove industry from 1830 to 1900. Later, they further refined the details of the bas-relief designs by switching to iron molds. They improved the casting process so the iron was smoother, thinner and subsequently lighter weight and could take on surface ornamentation. Since the heating stoves were to sit in people's parlors and bedrooms, they could not be big black iron monstrosities but needed to be tasteful— like pieces of sculpture. In so doing, manufacturers and their designers relied on cast iron's ease of bas-relief decoration. Simple decoration also served a functional purpose: it disguised some of the imperfections that are unavoidable when casting stove plate. Stove patternmakers selected designs to capture the spirit of the times—like the opening of the Erie Canal or Perry's victory in the War of 1812.

Intellectuals found stove decorations "ugly and contemptible." But fortunately for the industry's prospects, its millions of customers paid no attention to their highbrow tastes and loved the stove designs.

The stove was really the very first mass-marketed, had-to-have durable good for American families. The market was wide open. Armies of traveling salesmen and agents hit the roads. The industry was competitive in the extreme, and designs and patented functional features were seen as the way to beat one's competitors. Harris reports in his article "Inventing the U.S. Stove Industry" that in the late 1840s the U.S. Patent Office recorded that almost 90 percent of all patents were issued for stoves, and it remained above 50 percent for the next decade. The following is a U.S. patent from 1887:

Cooking at Home

The design for a stove-top ornament, consisting of the pedestal, the cup, having cherubic figures, the brackets surmounted by animal-heads in newt [neat] delineation, the column, with the bulb and button and inverted bottle shaped ornamentation all having the shape and ornamentation as shown.

Detroit stove manufacturers displayed their stoves during the 1869 Michigan State Fair, where thirty thousand people passed through the "Domestic Hall" to see rows of working stoves, whose "infernal heat made the place anything but comfortable for the inmates," as reported by the *Detroit Free Press*. But the cooking stoves were loved.

Miss Maria Parloa was a bestselling cookbook author and co-founder of *Ladies Home Journal*. In 1880, Parloa captured the general feeling:

So near perfection have the makers of ranges and stoves come that it would be difficult to speak of possible improvements, especially in stoves....No single piece of furniture contributes so much to the comfort of a family as the range or stove, which should, therefore, be the best of its kind.

Of course, not everyone thought stoves were a good idea. Traditionalists had a lukewarm response to the change in the home. Albert Bolles, an early historian of the stove industry, wrote in 1879, "The open fire was the true centre of home-life, and it seemed perfectly impossible to everybody to bring up a family around a stove."

Catharine Beecher was well known in the United States through her writing, tours and visits. She was a fierce advocate for women's rights in the home and for wholesome living. She worked tirelessly for education on the western frontier. Her sister was Harriet Beecher Stowe, the author of *Uncle Tom's Cabin*, and her brother, Henry Ward Beecher, was equally well known as an abolitionist and social reformer. Catharine Beecher saw creeping evil in the stove's flue design in contrast to the wholesomeness of traditional fireplaces. She was especially concerned with proper venting of stoves' fumes. She and her sister Harriet wrote that the stove could cause nothing less than "moral insanity." The Stowes stated in their book *The American Woman's Home* (1869) that keeping one's home warm with a poorly vented stove was like putting one's family "in the Black Hole of Calcutta."

Catherine's romantic traditionalism saw no place for stoves:

Catharine Esther Beecher (September 6, 1800–May 12, 1878) was an American educator known for her forthright opinions on female education.

In these days, how common is it to provide rooms with only a flue for a stove!…Better, far better, the old houses of the olden time, with their great roaring fires, and their bed-rooms where the snow came in and the wintry winds whistled. Then, to be sure, you froze your back while you burned your face, your water froze nightly in your pitcher, your breath congealed in ice-wreaths on the blankets, and you could write your name on the pretty snow-wreath that had sifted in through the window-cracks. But you woke full of life and vigor, you looked out into the whirling snow-storms without a shiver, and thought nothing of plunging through drifts as high as your head on your daily way to school. You jingled in sleighs, you snow-balled, you lived in snow like a snow-bird, and your blood coursed and tingled, in full tide of good, merry, real life, through your veins—none of the slow-creeping, black blood which clogs the brain and lies like a weight on the vital wheels!

Apparently, few agreed with Mrs. Beecher, as stoves sold in the millions. As Mr. Harris reports, they began to penetrate homes from the 1820s to the Civil War and sold in the South once the war ended. In 1860, over one million stoves were made and sold, and in 1870, two million were sold. Every fourth American household by that time had a stove.

COOKING ON YOUR NEW STOVE

Cooking on a coal- or wood-burning stove was not simple. One did not increase the heat by adding more fuel; instead, one manipulated a complex collection of "checks, dampers, and draughts." Opening or closing them controlled the heat of the fire.

In her book *Guide for Young Housekeepers*, published in 1894, Maria Parloa walks us through the firing-up process that thousands of women did on a daily basis:

> *In the morning remove all the ashes and cinders. Put the shavings or paper on the grate loosely, then put in the kindling wood...Open all the draughts and light the fire. As soon as the wood begins to burn put on some coal. Let it burn for ten minutes then open the dampers...Fill the fire box and when all the coal is burning close the draughts...when you do not require a hot fire open all the checks. When you want a hot fire close the checks and open the draughts, and of course the moment there is no need of a fire, close the draughts and open the checks again. A fire built and managed in this manner can be used constantly for four to five hours.*

Cookstoves were not complete unless they were attached to a chimney or flue. The fire was kindled at the bottom of the stove, where the cold air entered the firebox. As the air was heated, it was pressed upward in the chimney, causing a draft. The cold air coming in at the bottom, in its turn, was heated and kept on this continuous upward push.

In the nineteenth century, chimneys frequently "smoked"; the smoke would not go up the chimney. There were several causes for smoky chimneys. Some had to do with the size, height, length and temperature of the chimney.

Also, on windy days it was not unusual in wood-burning stoves to notice the frightening sight of flames roaring out through the openings of the stove. Such conditions were usually caused by a poor chimney. As one cookbook in 1902 by Sarah Tyson Rorer explained:

A general store selling Garland stoves. *U.S. Library of Congress.*

An ordinary cookstove with such a draft would, on a quiet day, bake beautifully, but never when the wind is blowing. Chimneys built on the south or east side of a house give less trouble than those on the west or north side. The cold air is apt to chill them.

THE STOVE INDUSTRY: ENTER DETROIT

The industry of manufacturing stoves began in New York. Albany was considered a good spot due to the high quality and availability of casting sand. American stoves had an excellent reputation, as reported in the *Albany Atlas* in 1853:

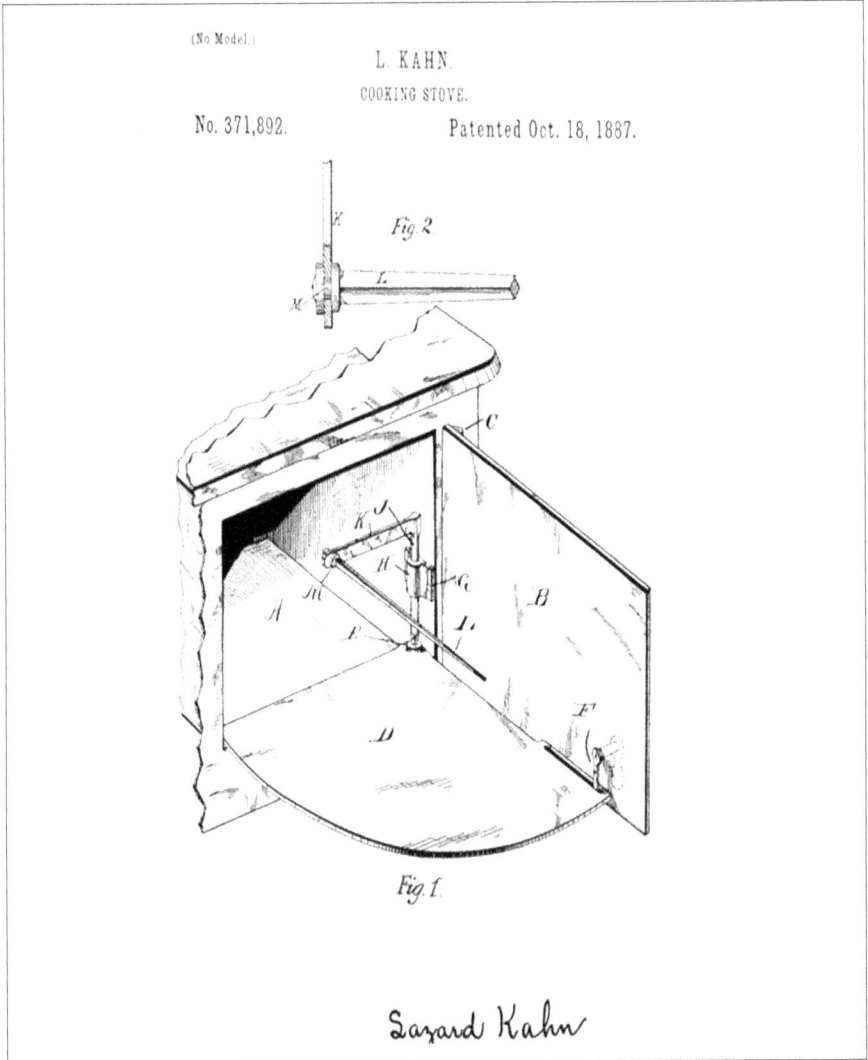

(No Model.)

L. KAHN.

COOKING STOVE.

No. 371,892.

Patented Oct. 18, 1887.

Fig. 2

Fig. 1

Sazard Kahn

A U.S. registered patent for a cooking stove apparatus.

The Atlas *learns that Rathbone and Co. have received an order for* *500 Albany cooking stoves for the Australian market…the English* *stoves are heavy, clumsy and costly…* [not] *easy for transportation into* *the interior, nor so easy for backwoodsmen or dwellers in tents as the* *Yankee contrivances.*

Stoves were soon made everywhere in the United States. Detroit entered the stove industry relatively late, in 1861. It took on stove manufacturing with passion and would eventually claim to be the "stove capital of the world." It began with Jeremiah Dwyer and his brother, James, who bought a reaper manufacturer that tried to build stoves and was facing bankruptcy. As Dwyer stated in an interview with the *Detroit Free Press* in 1906 after he retired, "The firm had been trying to make reapers and stoves. Never a more unwise match. The sort of iron used for reapers is exactly the opposite the kind for stoves."

Dwyer built his first simple four-burner cookstove, which he called the Defiance. Dwyer was a true workaholic. He began with a crew of fifty, and at dawn he helped to cast the iron and assemble stoves. At night, he delivered finished stoves to retailers or agents in Detroit. After hours, he walked through the plant as the factory night watchman and slept in a small wooden house next to the manufactory.

By the 1870s, Detroit had several large stove manufacturers: Detroit Stove Company, Michigan Stove Company, the Art Stove Company and the Detroit Vapor Stove Company. By 1908, there were twelve companies manufacturing stoves that employed 7,500 people. Detroit was consuming eighty thousand tons of iron to produce 450,000 "regular" (wood, coal and coke) stoves and ranges and 250,000 gas stoves.

Regions of the United States and sometimes very small areas needed special accommodations for a stove to make it work properly. In the earliest few years of natural gas–fueled stoves, the gas pressure could be uneven in different areas of the country. Houses built on hillsides had to deal with winds that produced odd drafts in the stove ventilation; some areas had only anthracite coal and others bituminous, and some had only wood. This developed in the big stove manufacturers a capability to accommodate tiny market segments and still make money. At the same time, the stove manufacturers differentiated their products through functional features such as plate warmers and boilers, but just as importantly appealed to the eye through decorative designs.

However, designs were regarded by the companies as seasonal, much like furniture or clothes fashions, and were short lived. As Dwyer stated:

> *The stove business is a hard one to handle. There is an immense amount of detail and one style follows another with rapidity. I often compare it to the millinery business. Patterns that sell well today have little or no demand next season; and there is endless rivalry bringing out new models.*

The results of all these continuously changing styles were enormous catalogues and increasing expense. Detroit Stove Works offered over eight hundred models, and Michigan Stove company had over seven hundred; these were typical of the book-sized catalogues of the times. According to an 1876 *Detroit Free Press*:

> *The Detroit Stove works yesterday shipped to Philadelphia their contribution to the Centennial Exhibition consisting of thirteen sample stoves...These will be set up on a raised and carpeted platform...On the lower edge of the platform are two beautiful cookstove, one for wood and the other for coal, named respectively "Telft" and "Occident"...Other stoves in this collection are "The Golden Age" a cookstove for either coal or wood; the "Gazelle", a parlor cookstove with illuminated front and hot blast attachment; "the Antelope" a cottage parlor stove...all these stoves are nickel plated and highly polished, the details on them are mechanically perfect...every stove looking almost too elegant for use.*

Americans were proud of their kitchen stoves. A hearth may have been homey, but the kitchen stove cooked food like the Michigan Marching Band. Consider the functionality of the kitchen stove compared to the old hearth. Even Catherine Beecher and Harriet Beecher Stowe were in awe of the cooking stove's capabilities:

> *With proper management of dampers, one ordinary-sized coal-hod of anthracite coal will, for twenty-four hours, keep the stove running, keep seventeen gallons of water hot at all hours, bake pies and puddings in the warm closet, heat flat-irons under the back cover, boil tea-kettle and one pot under the front cover, bake bread in the oven, and cook a turkey in the tin roaster in front.*

There were no thermometers yet for ovens, and thermostats did not make an appearance until 1913, so the home cook had to come up with some method to determine when an oven was at the right temperature to bake a cake or set custard. One method involved having white paper nearby. A piece of paper was put on the bottom of the oven. Maria Parloa explains a system in her book *New Cook Book and Marketing Guide*: "For pastry the oven should be hot enough to turn the paper dark brown in five minutes...for bread six minutes. For cupcakes an oven should turn the paper dark yellow in five minutes."

A woman standing beside her stove.

Cookbooks quickly adapted. New recipes for soufflés, tarts, pies and cakes appeared that would have been difficult or impossible in a hearth. And there was even a debate about the loss of flavor of food cooked in a stove oven versus a hearth. What cast-iron cooking range could touch Mrs. Leslie's gridiron steaks? The new ovens had no broilers. Cookbooks as late as 1885 referred to a steak cooked in a cast-iron oven as "baked beef." To achieve roasted meats, a device called a "tin kitchen" was set before a fireplace.

Cooking stoves also spawned a popular trend of cooking schools that began in the 1860s and peaked in the 1880s. As cooking stoves became popular, American women were accused of not knowing how to use them. It was argued that they used far too much coal and cooked at temperatures that were too high. According to the *New York Times* in 1895:

Having coal in abundance the iron stove has held sway, while we have grossly maltreated the finest products in the world by subjecting them to the heat of the "American frying pan" thus rendering them indigestible, and unfit for human stomachs. Italians and French are proverbially good cooks. Their methods are gingerly compared to our American ways.

Of course, a stove did not spell the end of hard work in the kitchen for women. A study of coal stoves was conducted in 1899, as reported by Susan Stasser in her book *Never Done* (coal would replace wood in the late nineteenth century). The study found that during a six-day period,

twenty minutes were spent in sifting ashes, fifteen minutes in carrying coal, and two hours and nine minutes on blacking the stove to keep it from rusting. [During those six days,] *292 pounds of new coal were put in the stove...27 pounds sifted out of the ashes, and more than 14 pounds of kindling* [were hauled].

To keep one fire burning through the winter required three to four tons of coal.

9

Cooking Lessons

"Oh," said a matronly lady, as she took a second spoonful of charlotte russe, "How I wish there had been such a chance to learn cooking when I first went to housekeeping. I nearly killed my husband with my experimental cooking."
—Detroit Free Press, *1884*

Cooking classes and demonstrations became popular in the 1870s and early 1880s as more and more Detroiters bought kitchen cookstoves. Although there were cookbooks based on hearth cooking, the first cooking instruction began in Detroit in the 1870s after cookstoves were commonly found in middle-class kitchens. Boston and New York had cooking schools a decade before Detroit; for example, in New York, a Frenchman named Pierre Blot, who became a national celebrity referred to as "Professor Blot," wrote books and began to teach cooking classes in 1865. These were written about in the Detroit newspapers.

Detroit cooking instruction didn't appear until several years later. In those days, a woman or girl who by age twelve could not cook could be subject to some severe and withering accusations. For many, it was a moral obligation neglected; a woman who could not cook for her family was "a very good example of a useless sort of woman." Here's a sample from the *Health Journal* of 1880: "Whether they are fine ladies or poor, working girls they should know that the women who cannot cook and serve up an appetizing meal without wasting good food is a disgrace to her sex."

In addition to taking care of a healthy family, many popular cookbook authors also wrote about cooking and caring for the sick and invalid, which was common for American families who looked after the elderly or infirm in their own homes. There could be a nurse's unsmiling sternness in recipes and cooking instructions. Temperance groups claimed that good cooking had redemptive powers, as in the following from the *Detroit Free Press* in 1896:

> *The daughter of a drunkard attended cooking school...and became quite proficient at making pastry. One day she told her father that she was going to make custard for supper and asked him to stay home instead of going to the saloon as he usually did. The father promised he would, but expressed some doubt about his little daughter's ability to make the custard...When he came home that evening he found a clean tablecloth, the dining room newly swept...a tidy homelike appearance...and among appetizing dishes the custard. That night he remained at home...he quit visiting the saloons all the result of his little daughter's making the custard as she had been taught to do in the church cooking school.*

There was only one salvation for the hapless young women: "she should not marry until she has qualified herself at the cooking school."

One of the first cooking teachers in Detroit was Matilda Lee Dods, who visited the city in 1876. Miss Dods was Scottish and, as announced in the newspapers, "has taken for her mission to teach her American sisters how to cook." She gave classes in several large American cities. She was actually an emissary of sorts, one of several, sent to the United States and Canada by the internationally recognized South Kensington Cooking School in London, England, of which she was a graduate. She held her classes at Detroit's St. Andrews Hall for "very large crowds," and according to another cooking teacher, Maria Parloa, she supposedly made "a small fortune" doing so. Notebooks and pencils were passed out to all attending so that they might be able to record every step of the process. In one class, it was reported that Miss Dods "roasted a chicken, made some milk rolls, dished up some railway pudding and macaroni and cheese, baked a rough cake, and displayed a soup she'd made previously." At the conclusion of the class, "a large number of ladies crowded the platform and plied Miss Dods with questions."

Certain organizations sponsored cooking classes as a form of charity—classes for children or for poor mothers. Classes were also offered to working-class women to train them as servants. In 1869, Pierre Blot offered classes in cooking

Cooking at Home

Maria Parloa (1843–1909) was an American author of books on cooking and housekeeping, the founder of two cooking schools, a noted lecturer on food topics and an important early figure in the "domestic science" (later home economics) movement.

with the brand-new science of canned foods "to become the benefactor of inexperienced housewives of limited means."

But classes for young, married or single women were very popular. Groups like the Working Women's Home Association began the Detroit Cooking School in 1880. They offered two sessions a day for women who paid tuition under the guidance of chef teacher Monsieur Emile Esperon, "an experienced French cook." So many of the attendees were schoolteachers that the Detroit Cooking School offered "afternoon sessions" that corresponded to their working day. At one of those afternoon sessions, Monsieur Esperon demonstrated how to cook "calf brains and tongue, lamb chops a la Demiduff, Florida Shortcake, and Charlotte Russe."

As the *Detroit Free Press* reported, "There is quite an interest nowadays in the method of preparing food. Cooking schools are being established in all the large cities and it is gratifying to know that Detroit is not behind the rest."

To promote the cooking school, after each morning lesson the school would take the cooked food prepared during class and offer lunches at reasonable rates upon request to offices all over the city. As the *Free Press* reported in 1880:

Active boys can be seen at all hours of the day hurrying with tin pails to appease hungry mortality. There's a great future in store for this business. If it [the school] *were connected with the Telephone Exchange, so that a person could yell into the instrument, "send me up some hot pancakes," what a handy thing it would be.*

MARIA PARLOA

At times, nationally famous cookbook authors and syndicated columnists would tour big cities, such as Detroit, giving cooking classes. One of the most popular teachers and writers on home economics was Miss Maria Parloa from New York and the Boston Cooking School. Miss Parloa was the food editor at *Good Housekeeping* for many years; she was very influential in the nineteenth and early twentieth centuries on all issues related to cooking and housekeeping. She was a founding partner in the magazine *Ladies Home Journal.* Her cookbooks were in print from the late 1870s to the 1920s; some of them had at least ten editions and sold nearly half a million copies.

Born in Massachusetts on September 25, 1843, she was orphaned early and began her career cooking in homes and hotels. Her first lecture on cooking was in 1876, and her books provide an understanding of women's work and their role in American homes during her days. She was an advocate for the latest technology and kitchen appliances to lessen the work in the kitchen. Her book *Miss Parloa's New Cookbook: A Guide to Marketing and Cooking,* published in 1884, provided information on kitchen furnishings, from stoves to refrigerators and other devices of the day, such as the tin kitchen, bird roaster, squash strainer, apple parer, spice box, rice mould and jagging iron, among others. She believed in seasonal cooking and provided seasonal bills of fare. Some of her fans believe her recipe for tomato chowder to be the first tomato soup recipe, but actually, the *Detroit Free Press* published a "tomato soup" recipe in 1870.

The following advertisement appeared in the *Detroit Free Press* in April 1884:

Cooking at Home

Lessons in Cooking
Miss Maria Parloa, of New York,
Will give a series of twelve demonstration lessons in cooking in Abstract
Hall corner of Griswold and Lafayette.

Miss Parloa's class in Detroit was heavily advertised and was attended by one hundred of the best ladies of Detroit; "sealskin and diamonds were everywhere visible." She was a large, handsome woman described as having a musical, easy voice, a strong chin and an authoritative air; "her long hands were ambidextrous as a musician's." She wore a checked gingham dress and white apron and worked with an assistant at a hot stove set up on the stage. She made green pea soup, white fish with tartar sauce and, for dessert, Charlotte Russe. The reporter seemed entranced with Miss Parloa. He described her whipping cream for the Charlotte: "Then she whipped up the cream to a sea of foam amid which she stood like another Aphrodite."

"You must stir this cream one way when you put in the flavoring," said the teacher. "Down hard and light up…one-two-three, one-two-three— short strokes!"

She was asked in an interview in 1884 what "class of people in America take the most interest in learning how to cook."

Her response: "The best. I sometimes think the more intellect and accomplishments a woman has the more she wants to excel in this womanly virtue."

A few years later, Miss Parloa scheduled a cooking class in Jackson, Michigan, but just as the classes began, a murder was committed in the city, and all the ladies opted to go to the court to watch the murder trial rather than attend Miss Parloa's class. The class was cancelled.

After the turn of the century, Detroit stove companies began holding free cooking classes. They used the classes to promote their gas ranges and would hold the classes in their showroom windows for people walking by.

JESSIE DeBOTH

Much later, in the late 1920s through the mid-1950s, another cooking entertainer would emerge: Jessie DeBoth. Jessie DeBoth was the cooking and homemaking maven of the Depression. She was a native of Green Bay,

Wisconsin, graduated from college in 1915 and got her culinary training at the Stout Institute of Menominee. She was tall at five-foot-ten, with "Titian" hair. She was immensely popular as she toured the country. She drew twenty-five thousand people in Chicago, with thousands more turned away, and twenty-eight thousand in New York at a filled Carnegie Hall. Local newspapers sponsored the shows for each city. In Detroit, the classes, which were more like shows, were billed as the Detroit News Cooking School featuring Jessie DeBoth. Detroiters attended by the thousands starting in 1929. These events took place at the Masonic Temple, where the stage was turned into a fully equipped kitchen facility, dining room and functioning laundry room.

Along with the shows, DeBoth had several cookbooks, radio shows and television spots (*Jessie's TV Notebook*) in the 1950s. She was so popular that later she was known as the woman with "seven million friends."

DeBoth's four-day presentations were a mixture of cooking demonstrations, household tips, flamboyant entrances and giveaways. Audience participation was a must. DeBoth would make audience members sing or dance on stage. She would give away pots and pans for young couples, "mothers of quintuplets" or the last seat in the auditorium. When she offered a prize to the tallest, thinnest old maid in the house, the women hesitated, so she said, "I'm an old maid, and I don't mind a bit." Samples of food wrapped in waxed paper were tossed out to the audience for refreshments. She cracked jokes and encouraged audiences to get silly with kitchen utensils. Local bands from whatever city she was in provided music, sing-alongs and amateur shows. She claimed her shows ran the entire range of homemaking, except for how to "wind the clock and put the cat out." She even gave advice on teeth: "If you're not true to them, they'll be false to you." Another piece of advice that was reported in a historic article in the *Detroit News* was that "great men have said that more marriages are ruined by bad cooking than through any other cause."

The crowds were mostly women, although there was always a "White Elephant" session to which women could bring the men in their lives. Masonic Temple was filled year after year. Admission was free in the early days, but in an effort to cut down on the long lines, DeBoth began charging thirty to forty cents. Even then, the theater was filled to capacity. Thousands were turned away, and on at least one occasion, lines were four abreast for two and a half blocks outside the auditorium. This was before the days of television and talk shows.

Twenty-five baskets of food were given away each session, as well as items donated by businesses. The 1929 program lists thirty contributing companies.

A sampling of these items includes an "iceless refrigerator"(1929), washing machines, electric ranges, rugs, dishes, flowers, roasters, ironers, waterless cookers and Hoover sweepers.

During the war years, fifty baskets of food were distributed, and DeBoth's cooking was geared to the war effort with its rationing. She said that the woman who feeds her family nutritiously is "just as patriotic as the riveter or shell filler. Well fed people maintain production and morale."

Like Maria Parloa, DeBoth was a firm believer in scientific cooking and modern methods. "Scientific homemaking has revolutionized woman's traditional job," she often remarked. "The old fashioned method of guessing amounts has now gone by the board. The up to date cook measures and weighs carefully. No more handful of this, a cupful [any cup] of that," she said in a 1928 interview. "The kitchen today is a far cry from the old fashioned one. The modern kitchen, or kitchenette if you prefer—is really a laboratory. It's scrupulously clean in all its appointments."

In the introduction to *Modernistic Recipe-Menu Book* (1929), she notes:

The business of homemaking is one which engages the attention of many million women in the United States. Yet it is only at the time of the present census-taking that the lawmakers have come to acknowledge it, and have consented to list every housewife as "homemaker" instead of "unemployed." This is real progress.

10

The Detroit Kitchen

Floor to Ceiling

T he extravagant Victorian dinner parties did not just happen by magic; the kitchen had to have all the right tools and guidance. Advice on how to equip one's kitchen was also frequently given. In 1884, Miss Maria Parloa wrote:

> *The housekeeper will find that there is continually something new to be bought. If there be much fancy cooking, there must be an ice cream freezer, jelly and charlotte russe moulds and many little pans and cutters. The right way is, of course, to get the essential articles first, and then, from time to time, to add those used in fancy cooking.*

The cooking stove changed everything, especially cooking with gas. Now women could cook, roast, broil and bake in so many different ways that there was a new excitement in the kitchen, and without the ashes or coal dust there was less drudgery. The kitchen was a more appealing place to work. From 1900 to 1910, there was double the number of articles in local newspapers on cooking and the kitchen than in the previous or the following decades. Recipes from countries other than France, England and Germany were beginning to appear in Detroit newspapers: Mexican enchiladas, Italian risotto with saffron, Chinese chop "sooy" and bird's nest soup and Indian curries. On top of that, the kitchen and home were seen by businesses as a consumer market for innovative products, whether appliances, gadgets or even lighting.

THE ICEBOX

In the first half of the nineteenth century, a non-mechanical refrigerator was patented that used ice in an insulated cabinet to keep dairy products cool. It was slow to catch on due to the expense of ice. However, in 1827, Nathaniel Wyeth of Massachusetts patented a device that could cut ice on a frozen lake. It was a plow-like blade with saw teeth. Hooked up to a horse, it could score a deep, straight line into even the thickest lake ice. Men followed up with iron bars to break the ice into blocks along the cut line. The blocks were floated to shore and then slid up makeshift ramps to boxcars on trains whose tracks followed the lakes. The price of ice fell 60 percent.

Small towns along train lines across the country cashed in on this new industry employed by farmers with little or nothing to do during the winter. They supplied refrigerated railroad boxcars (invented in Detroit) with blocks of ice for shipment to icehouses that were holding stations for cargoes destined for homes and businesses. With no other way to keep perishables cool and fresh during hot weather, private homes, as well as businesses handling fresh foods, used insulated iceboxes (called refrigerators at the time; the "icebox" was only the chamber that held the ice), which held one to several blocks of ice to keep food safe from spoilage. Like the milkman, the ice man delivered block ice house to house. Maria Parloa wrote in 1884:

> *The trouble with most refrigerators is that the food kept in them is apt to have a peculiar taste. This is owing in a great measure to the wood used in the construction of the interior and for the shelves. On the inside of the Eddy chest-shaped refrigerator there is not a particle of wood, and the food kept in it is always sweet. It is simply a chest, where the ice is placed on the bottom and slate shelves put on top. With this style of refrigerator the waste of ice is much greater than in those built with a separate compartment for ice, but the food is more healthful.*

The early refrigerators were equipped with drinking faucets and, like today, dispensed icy cold water; however, back then, the water was meltwater from the ice block, which was formerly lake water or stagnant pond water. This was quickly seen as not a good idea and was discontinued. Other features included ice chambers located above or on the sides of the "provision chamber"; linings of white porcelain, which was much fancier than traditional galvanized sheet metal; and automatic drain traps to reduce "impure gases" rising back into

Ice harvest on a lake, circa 1905. *U.S. Library of Congress.*

the ice chamber. It was recommended that the refrigerator be cleaned once a week and that "brides be discouraged from buying elaborate refrigerators." One columnist from the *Detroit Free Press* in 1916 advised young brides, "Fancy furniture is quite appropriate for the drawing room...but the kitchen must be utterly devoid of all frills and fancies."

The kitchen was a place of duty, not pleasure. A modest refrigerator could be purchased for six to ten dollars in 1915.

COOKWARE

Popular cookware of the 1920s was enamelware—enameled steel. White with blue trim was very popular. But some kitchens had unique Detroit cookware made by Stroh's Beer. Stroh had a casting division that made automotive parts. In 1922, Stroh decided to produce cast-aluminum cookware. It called it Stroluminium. Stroluminium was extra heavy-duty cookware that included other items such as water kettles.

KITCHEN GADGETS

A Dover egg beater, one of the most common home-cooking tools one hundred years ago.

The first egg beaters appeared in the 1850s, and since that time more than one thousand patents have been awarded for different designs. Dover egg beaters came in three sizes and were so popular that at one point the generic term "dovering eggs" was used to describe the egg beating process in recipes. Fannie Merritt Farmer wrote, "Beat cream and eggs using the smallest sized Dover Egg Beater."

In Victorian Detroit, as elsewhere in the country, stands, forms and molds were common accessories; many dishes were not complete unless served in a recognizable, traditional shape. A cookbook on cooking and giving dinners by Mary Newton Foote Henderson called *Practical Cooking and Dinner Giving* (1877) shows molds with text for old favorites such as Charlotte Russe, blanc mange and molded meat pies.

Whole dinners were sometimes molded, as in one chicken dinner with rice.

One couldn't just serve fried smelt in a basket; smelt needed a display.

Meat molds and meat pie recipes were also popular. This used the calf's head meat, tongue and other meats set in pastry crusts, then molded and baked.

Cooking at Home

The Modern Kitchen

The design and materials used in the kitchen began to appear in the paper and magazines. A range-top stove was preferred because it was operated against a wall instead of away from it, providing more room. Another innovation was the Hoosier Kitchen Cabinet (or "Hoosier"), which was, according to its promoter in Detroit, "one of the most important steps in making the kitchen scientific." It was a kind of all-in-one unit with a cabinet, small cupboards, bins for flour and a working tabletop.

The Lowly Kitchen Floor

Flooring in kitchens was a concern. Kitchen floors needed to be solid to support the intense weight of a cast-iron cookstove. In the past, Georgia pine was commonly found in Detroit kitchens. The pine splintered and would "lip" or rise up at the tongue and groove seams. It was also stained from grease and would sometimes rot if kept too wet; that was a serious problem since rats would then get under the floor and into the kitchen. Stone was viewed as too hard and merciless on the cook's feet. Brick was somewhat less hard but cracked over time. Floorboards, either pine or maple, had a tendency to rot and stain. Tile was beautiful; white was especially prized, but it was expensive and, like stone, "tiresome to the feet," as reported by a *Detroit Free Press* review in 1922.

One new alternative available in the 1890s was oilcloth. The earliest oilcloth was canvas, waxed or oiled with linseed oil. Later, it was painted with lead, white or enamel, usually "light colors," and then decorated with patterns; the thicker the canvas and paint, the better. It was cheap and usually made with old sailing ship canvas, which was in abundance since wind sailing was no longer done much. Canvas makers searched for new markets and went from sailing to flooring. It had to be kept clean and dry but was durable and easier on the feet. To apply it, one tore up the pine boards (one Detroit family found thirty dead rats under the kitchen floor). Next, the dirt beneath the floor was dug out and "cleaned and purified" or replaced and raked evenly. Joists of hardwood such as hickory were put down with the bark on, as it preserved them a bit longer from rot. The space between the joists was filled with cartloads of clinkers—the remains of burned coal that had sharp edges like broken glass and effectively prevented the ingress of rats. The pine boards were replaced, but if lipped, edges of the boards had to be planed for the oilcloth to lie flat without gaps. A paper layer was put down, and then oilcloth was stretched and tacked over the boards.

Oilcloth was very popular. One columnist quoted a housewife as saying, "When it's cleaned it looks clean." It was replaced in the 1890s by synthetic flooring. The earliest version was "kamptulicon," which was a precursor of linoleum. Kamptulicon from the 1840s was ground cork sprinkled over strands of heated India rubber and then coated with linseed oil. It made a sensation at the International Exhibit of 1842 in London. It was also manufactured by machines, which was an innovation. However, it was too expensive, and when the price of India rubber went through the roof, the kamptulicon was kaput.

Linoleum appeared originally made of ground cork mixed with treated linseed oil and applied to canvas or burlap. It was invented in England in 1855. When linseed oil was heated, it became a very thick, tough, rubbery varnish. Pigments were added for color and patterns. By the 1920s, linoleum was the flooring of choice.

THE CEILING

Ceilings were painted before the plaster had dried, ensuring a good color not destroyed by flies. Walls had wainscoting and washable wood paneling that rose from the floor to a height of six feet to prevent permanent grease stains. Some exclusive houses had kitchens divided into "double rooms"; the range was put in a separate outer room with a flue pipe running from the range to the chimney. The following was described is an "ideal kitchen" by the *Detroit Free Press in* 1896:

> *In both kitchens was a white porcelain sink…with rows of hooks for pots and pans and bright copper articles. On the shelf over the sink in the inner kitchen stood lamps…kept cleaned and trimmed and filled. The corresponding sink in the outer kitchen was used for dishwashing and general kitchen work. Over this sink hung the skillets and stew pans…In the adjoining pantry were places for flour and grains, for the bread and cake*

and pies; a refrigerator for meat and one for butter and milk…In the outer kitchen were sofas and rocking chairs seldom used until after dark; also a hanging lamp over the range and the table;…the whole place looked then more a fairy laboratory for the making of flowers than a common kitchen for cooking meats.

PESTS IN THE KITCHEN

In the nineteenth century, few things drove people crazier than houseflies for a couple of reasons. First, there were billions of them, many more than today. With horses everywhere, there was horse manure everywhere, which was perfect for flies and maggots. One post office in Jackson, Michigan, estimated that it had a million flies in it over a summer. Detroit alleys were thick with flies. Everybody had manure boxes, but many never cleaned them, and very few even covered them. Garbage and refuse was left in open containers or simply dumped on the ground, and garbage collection never happened. Many Detroiters solved the problem of the alleys by building tall plank fences, which did nothing to prevent their homes from filling up with flies. The second reason flies were much worse in the kitchen was that there were no screens on windows. Metallic screens were invented well after the Civil War and did not appear in Detroit retail stores until 1882. Besides being an obnoxious nuisance, flies were dangerous, carrying over one hundred pathogens commonly found in nineteenth-century Detroit, such as typhoid, cholera, salmonella, dysentery, tuberculosis and parasitic worms.

The only hope one had was poison or flypaper. Flypaper was made to order at local drugstores.

Poison was dangerous, but flypaper was nasty stuff. It was invented in 1840. Sticky, smelling goop irresistible to houseflies was painted onto strips of paper and then hung in the kitchen. The problem in the early days was that the goop soaked through the paper and sometimes dripped off, and it did not last; in a couple days, it hardened and had to be replaced. During the early 1880s, a Grand Rapids druggist, William Thum, assigned the task of making flypaper for customers to his four sons, Otto, Hugo, William and Ferdinand. It was a tedious, nasty job, but it gave the clever brothers time to figure out ways to improve the sticky formula and the application process.

An advertising piece for Tanglefoot flypaper.

They came up with a formula based on castor oil, resins and wax that had a much longer shelf life and didn't saturate the paper backing. Tanglefoot flypaper was born. Several other companies produced flypaper, but none was as well known as Tanglefoot. The Tanglefoot formula was patented in 1887. The Thums launched a plant in Grand Rapids and soon were shipping flypaper around the world.

RATS!

Today, most people would not even enter a house that had a rat roaming around, but at one time when a house was described as "infested with rats," it was not good but not unusual. There was nothing that rats would not go after in a kitchen. The following is an example from the *Detroit Free Press* of 1873: "The rats gnawed through a lead pipe in a house on Howard street Thursday night and yesterday the kitchen was found ankle deep in water. Damage was occasioned to the amount of $25."

Many women kept eggs in a basket on the countertop. Rats were known to steal off the counter a dozen whole eggs without a trace; months later, the eggs would be found whole and uncracked under the floor or in a wall. People wondered how rats even carried eggs let alone got them down from a countertop. There were regular international theories and debates about how rats pulled off this trick, with poultry farmers among the particularly interested. No less a person than naturalist John Burroughs wrote about the mystery in *Scientific American* (he said he had no idea). Some people (mostly men) stayed up entire nights to witness this weird event and solve this puzzler of ages. It was unofficially solved and published in the *New York Times, London Times* and many more newspapers. Here is one of many *Detroit Free Press* articles on the issue in 1903:

> *These eye witnesses of a most unusual thing say the rat holds the egg between its chin and forefeet or hugged tightly between the forefeet; that he tumbles off elevations deftly protecting the egg as he falls; that there is usually a crowd of rats about to drag the egg rat on his back by the tail to the rat hole...It is agreed that rats work in gangs when egg carrying...and there is always much squealing.*

An advertising piece for Rough on Rats rat poison.

However, a true fear—a gnawing fear—was rats crawling in walls with wooden kitchen matches sticking out of their mouths that would scratch against stone, a pipe or cement and ignite, putting the house in flames. This happened. In kitchens, rats were a menace. In addition, since many women did the laundry in the kitchen, as well, the rats presented a serious threat to the family.

Some experts, such as Dr. Henry Leffmann, a sanitary chemist "of unique attainments," recommended pouring floors of concrete, radical for the times. He and others suggested building kitchens on the second floor of the house, away from the damp root cellars. Detroit's own health officer, William H. Price, pushed through an ordinance in 1917 that forbade living in root cellars and mandated that all new buildings had to construct "rat-proof" cellars.

The pesticide of the day for rats was Rough on Rats, which had the slogan "Don't die in the house"; this was an obnoxious and dangerous problem, with rats crawling under the floor or into walls to die.

In the 1880s, a destitute New Jersey pharmacist had only one thing that kept him and his wife from starvation: a single loaf of bread. The story goes that in the morning, they found their bread had been eaten by rats. The man, Ephraim S. Wells, vowed to devote his life to destroy this enemy. Whether or not the story is true, Wells invented a product that did just that, and in four years he became a millionaire. His wife called it Rough on Rats; the name stuck, and the product was a huge success. Business historians consider Rough on Rats to be one of the first products to succeed purely through advertising. Wells spent a fortune on advertising. He even wrote sheet music for a Rough on Rats song that he marketed. Rough on Rats also claimed to rid your house of mice, roaches, flies, beetles, moths, ants, skunks, weasels, gophers, moles and muskrats. His rat poison sold around the world.

However, there was a dark side to this story. Chemists of the day analyzed the product and found it contained nearly pure arsenic. It could be bought by anyone of any age at any drugstore; some country pharmacists claimed to sell one ton a year. It started a disturbing trend: suicide by poisoning. In 1888, Australian chemists reported five suicides and one attempt in less than one month from Rough on Rats. In American cities, this became nearly a daily tragedy in the 1880s. Rough on Rats was also used for murders, as it arrived on the market at the same time personal life insurance came into being. It was called the "inheritance powder" in England. Newspapers claimed the product killed more people than rats, and governments around the world called for a ban on the product or at least restricted access.

The rat problem in Detroit was rooted in the alleys. Every five years starting in the 1880s, Detroit would declare a "War on Rats!" But rats were everywhere, and many people just took them as part of living. A study on U.S. rat damage in 1907 estimated that rats destroyed $200 million worth of foodstuffs every twelve months. In 1920, real estate companies in Detroit brought in a superstar rat exterminator from Pittsburgh who, after three months of assessing the situation, wrote a letter to the editor of the *Free Press* in 1912:

> *Detroit has more than its full share of rats…I find that Detroit is badly infested. I base my claim on personal observation of every part of your city…Most of the people here do not seem to mind the rats at all. I have come to the conclusion that Detroit would be lonesome without them…It seems passing strange that the most beautiful city in the United States would tolerate such conditions…The source of the rats—the alleys!*

People driving down alleys at night saw thousands of rats.

The Russell House, the hallowed hotel of old Detroit, had a twelve-pound cat that was owned by the chef to keep the building free of rats. Others were not so fortunate; some country inns in the Midwest were not only infested but also absolutely taken over by rats to the point that they had to be abandoned. Rats devoured entire animals. They seemed to have a love of piglets' tails. Farmers would find entire herds of pigs with tails eaten by rats.

Some hotels, restaurants and occasionally homeowners hired professional rat catchers. Rat catchers of the day were hired in Detroit by hotels, stables, warehouses, homes or any entity that had food or goods of interest to rats. One rat catcher said that in three nights he had driven 217 rats from a "private residence." In 1878, the Detroit newspapers reported that the city hall basement was infested with "fat and ferocious rats."

The rat catchers many times worked in teams. Some worked alone using ferrets or weasels to find and drive the rats from the floors, walls and crevices of old buildings. In a few days, they could drive hundreds of rats out of hotels and into their traps. Rat catchers were quite proud of their trade, as one who was interviewed in Detroit in 1899 shows:

> "When a man starts in as a professional rat-catcher and gets to understand training ferrets there is such an attraction he never willingly give it up. It is a profitable business."
>
> "Do the ferrets ever bite?"
>
> "It's a very careless and awkward man who gets bitten by a trained ferret. When one is bitten by an enraged ferret the bite is of a very severe character, is extremely painful and slow to heal…Of course, we generally muzzle them when we send them in after rats."
>
> They began by locating every rat hole throughout the building and placing traps or special sacks around each. Ferrets were kept hungry for a few days before the job to give them a keen gleam in their eye as the rat catcher sent the ferrets into the walls driving the game before them, out of the holes and into the bags.
>
> "When a ferret is full grown and has the skill and courage that he should have, he is a holy terror to rats."

Some rat catchers used only their wits and a little poison. Here, a reporter worked alongside a professional rat catcher at a carriage house:

> The rat catcher wore a pair of light cloth slippers, heavy trousers, flannel shirt and vest. He had a kit of tools with him…First he went around the

edges of the floor and learned every rat hole...he then took a number of little wire doors out of his bag. They were four inches square. These he screwed into the edge of the holes so that the rat could easily get out but when the door fell shut he could not get back in... "Phosphorous poison causes the most horrid thirst. They'll come out to drink, I assure you." [The rat-catcher] *was now moving about in a most stealthy manner; now trying one little gate and now another. He lighted a stub pipe and perched himself at the bottom of a step ladder with his chin in his hand. Everything was quiet for a few minutes then there was a slight scratching at one of the doors, and a monstrous rat slowly came out. The door dropped to behind him and...he ran squealing along the wall.*

"He's a good one," remarked the little man in a whisper. "Tell you what I'll do, I'll catch this one with my hands."

He began to squeak through his teeth and slowly approach the fat intruder. The rat backed into a corner his little eyes gleaming and his tail swishing rapidly from side to side...In an instant the little man had sprung forward with a bound that was entirely reckless and went head first for the rat. Both hands were outstretched and he pinned it to the floor with a force that made it squeal.

"He is indeed a fat one, sir," getting to his feet. "You can observe—

"Keep him away!"

Much Ado about Mutton

Home Cooking

It was common in the early nineteenth century for travelers from Europe, especially England, France and Germany, to visit cities throughout the country, including Detroit, and write about their experiences for sophisticated urbane audiences in London, Paris or Berlin. Among the commentators was Charles Dickens, author Harriet Martineau and Mrs. Francis Trollope, mother of Victorian English novelist Anthony Trollop. Sometimes, wealthy New Yorkers would join in on this bashing, the tone usually mocking and condescending. Of the crude frontier behavior, nothing seemed to provoke more ridicule than "domestic manners," which included the food Americans ate, the speed and gross quantities we consumed and the overall horrible table manners. The food was generally condemned as "a monotonous round of badly cooked food."

Especially vicious was a French traveler, C.F. Volney. In his book from 1804, he said that

> *they* [Americans] *live in a state of habitual indigestion...I will venture to say that if a prize were proposed for the scheme of a regimen most calculated to injure the stomach, the teeth, and the health in general, no better could be invented than that of the Americans diet.*

And the results were tragic according to Volney:

Travelers are equally agreed on the frequency of defluxions on the gums, rottenness of teeth, and the premature loss of these valuable instruments of mastication. It is particularly lamentable to observe…handsome young women, from the age of fifteen or twenty have their teeth disfigured with black spots and frequently a great part of them gone.

In Detroit and surrounding areas, there was some truth to this. In the 1810s through the 1850s, more and more Yankee emigrants from New York and New England poured into Detroit. Many remained in Detroit, but more settled on farms in surrounding villages or moved throughout the state. They cleared land, built log homes and began farms. Settlers talked about the "Michigan appetite," which was a condition of being perpetually hungry. The settlers' diet was limited in the extreme. People might go six months without salt. Meat was infrequently eaten.

One man named A.D.P. Van Buren writing in 1884 recalled his days as a boy in a log cabin. He described his mother hanging iron pots on the crane or hook suspended over the fire in the hearth. When they had meat, such as pork or chicken, they were sometimes held on a wire before the fire to roast. Baking was done in a "tin reflector" or, if lucky, a separate side baking oven also in the chimney. But for the most part, there was very little to eat. The larder usually had only wheat, corn, pork and potatoes: "Pink-eyes" and "Meshanics" were the potato varieties. There was no fruit except wild plums or berries. The meal was typically bread, pork and potatoes. There was seldom tea, sugar or coffee. Settlers made what they called "crust coffee" out of browned wheat grains.

Van Buren described a meal:

The usual meal began with a platter of potatoes piled up steaming hot and placed on the center of the table; bread or Johnny-cake [a hard corn biscuit]; perhaps some meat boiled or fried; and an article largely partaken of was a bowl of flour gravy, looking like starch and made something like it, of flour and water, with a little salt and sometimes enriched with meat gravy.

While the dinner was modest, the people were generally happy. Relatives were typically on farms up the road or nearby. Sometimes, fellow settlers

VEAL.

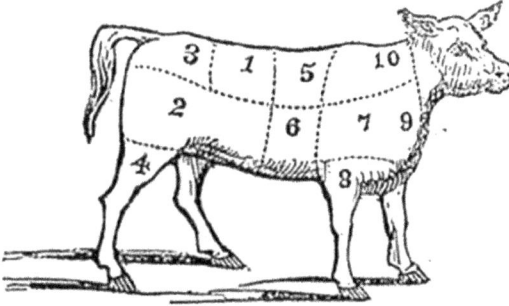

1. Loin, Best End.
2. Fillet.
3. Loin, Chump End.
4. Hind Knuckle.
5. Neck, Best End.

6. Breast, Best End.
7. Blade Bone, or Oyste
8. Fore Knuckle.
9. Breast, Brisket End.
10. Neck, Scrag End.

PORK.

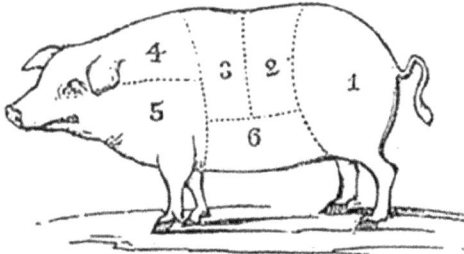

1. Leg.
2. Hind Loin.
3. Fore Loin.

4. Spare Rib.
5. Hand.
6. Belly, or Spring.

Pierre Blot's diagram on cuts of meat for the home cook. *Special Collections, Michigan State University Libraries.*

A clapboard farmhouse, 1942. *Michigan Historical Museum Archive.*

worked cooperatively for barn or roof raisings or "bees," such as logging bees, threshing bees, husking bees or quilting bees.

A farmer would walk from cabin to cabin to invite the neighbors to his raising or bee. Some cabins could be twenty miles apart. Van Buren recalled farmers out until midnight walking the neighborhood circuit, but Van Buren added, "The cheering response you got at every cabin, *'I'll be there to help you,'* sent you on your way rejoicing."

Of course, the neighbors working all day expected to be fed at dinnertime. One writer, Henry Ormal Severance, described in his book, *Michigan Trailmakers*, a log cabin dinner held for neighbors in Commerce Township in West Bloomfield. A young woman named Louisa, age seventeen, made the dinner, which consisted of mashed potatoes, boiled chicken and hot chicken gravy with biscuits floating on top. As the writer recalls:

Johnnie was a devout Methodist and when he asked [to say] the blessing at the table he had the habit of bending forward, dropping his face an inch or two over his plate. Charles...moved the bowl of gravy and biscuits in front of Johnnie at the very moment his head dropped forward. His nose dropped into the hot soup. He started to say "Our Father"—and ended with "Gosh darn it! It's hot!" to the amusement of all the men. The whole table was in an uproar.

FRENCH DETROIT HAD IT TOGETHER

Of course, in Detroit, where the French inhabitants, or *habitans*, had been cultivating farms for over one hundred years by 1800, they had fruit, vegetables, wine, cider and more. The local farmers maintained "ribbon farms," which were extremely narrow (only a few hundred feet wide) but very deep (up to three miles long), giving each person access to the waterways. Each farm had a house, log at first and then later covered with whitewashed boards. They were abundant farms with unique produce, such as yellow turnips and a variety of apple strains, including the Calville Blanc d'Hiver and the Detroit Red. Detroit was famous for its magnificent pear trees that rose as high as sixty feet and looked stunning in the spring covered with white blossoms. The original seeds were said to have been brought over from France. According to local historian and French Canadian descendant Ralph Naveaux:

Legend has it that the pear trees were planted in groups of 12, representing the apostles, with one set apart in memory of Judas's betrayal. A few descendants of the original trees can still be found in private holdings around the county [Monroe]. Ironically, they are the result of graftings taken from an ancient "Judas" tree discovered in Detroit's Waterworks Park in the 1970s or 80s.

French farm wives maintained their vegetable gardens and would sit in front of the farmers' markets selling produce. Their husbands and sons were outdoorsmen and supplemented the table with venison, bear, frog legs from the Lake St. Clair Flats, muskrat, whitefish, walleye and wild birds.

Cooking from Scratch

Of course, as settlers' farms prospered, the dinners went beyond pork, bread and gravy. Since most people in nineteenth-century Detroit lived on farms, the cookbooks and recipes of the day reflected the fact that the reader raised her own food. What did that mean for the farm wife as she opened her cookbook to plan the Sunday feast? For starters, it meant telling her husband to sharpen his axe and head to the barn, or perhaps she went out herself. To make some of the recipes would require a three-week rest after dinner. This is Pierre Blot's recipe from a popular cookbook sold in Detroit in 1867:

To Scald a Suckling Pig
The moment the pig is killed, put it into cold water for a few minutes; then rub it over with a little resin beaten extremely small, and put it into a pail of scalding water half a minute: take it out, lay it on a table, and pull off the hair as quickly as possible.

Sarah Josepha Buell Hale wrote *The Good Housekeeper, or The Way to Live Well and to Be Well While We Live*. Her cookbooks, which were popular in Detroit, went even further, telling housewives how to raise animals for the tastiest results:

Pork that is fed from the dairy, and fattened on corn is the best—potatoes do very well for part of the feeding. But pork fattened from the still-house is all but poisonous; it should never be eaten by Christians or those who wish to preserve their health.

Eat Anything and Cook Everything on It

Later in the twentieth century, Detroiters and Americans in general would turn up their noses at organ meats and tough cuts of meat, but a century before that, people did not have that luxury and relished the variety. Women cooked everything and seemed to enjoy it, despite hours of hard labor.

Calf's head was commonly used for mock turtle soup but also was a centerpiece dish. Sometimes meat was removed for salads or luncheons. Everybody on farms had extra calves (males; you only needed one bull), so veal was cheaper than chicken. Here is the start of a *Detroit Free Press* recipe from 1877 for mock turtle soup:

> *Split open the head and remove the brains and tongue, chop off the teeth and take out the eyes; soak, wash and scrub the head thoroughly; boil in eight quarts of water with salt, removing scum as it rises.*

Mrs. Maria Rundell's cookbook, *A New System of Domestic Cookery*, was published in 1807. Here is Mrs. Rundell's recipe for pig's cheeks:

> TO PREPARE PIG'S CHEEKS
> *Cut off the snout, and clean the head; divide it, and take out the eyes and the brains; sprinkle the head with salt, and let it drain twenty-four hours. Salt it with common salt and saltpeter: let it lie eight or ten days if to be dressed without stewing with peas, but less if to be dressed with peas; and it must be washed first, and then simmered till all is tender.*

LOST DETROIT DESSERTS

Another dish served for over one hundred years was the dessert blancmange. Blancmange was essentially almond-flavored Jell-O. It was made with milk or cream and sugar thickened with gelatin or cornstarch and often flavored with almonds. It was usually set in a mold and served cold and was considered light and refreshing.

A dessert that appears in every cookbook for one hundred years is Charlotte Russe. A Charlotte was a molded dessert lined with cookies or strips of cake and filled with fruit and vanilla pudding. Charlotte Russe was a dessert invented by the French chef Marie Antoine Carême (1784–1833), who named it in honor of his Russian employer Czar Alexander I (*Russe* is the French word for "Russian"). It is a cold dessert of Bavarian cream set in a mold lined with Ladyfingers.

But the dessert favored by Detroit men was pie. Bakers couldn't bake enough pie for Detroit men. The overall most popular type of pie was lemon meringue. It had to have a huge pile of white meringue on top. Cooking school instructors visiting Detroit complained to the *Detroit Free Press* in 1907:

> *"Whenever I go," said a cooking teacher who recently visited Detroit, "I get more requests for lemon meringue pie than anything else. No, they seldom ask me for bread and when I give a bread talk its almost always empty seats. A pie talk is always well attended, and the women confess to me nearly always that they are awfully anxious to learn to make a real good pie 'because my husband does love it so.'"*

SUNDAY DINNER

Some dishes that Detroiters ate regularly are long gone today. One of the most popular Sunday dinners was roast mutton. Mutton is sheep and was cheaper than lamb. It had a strong, wooly taste, which some disliked, but one butcher from Walled Lake said in the 1870s that if you skinned the sheep right, "it would not taste of the wool." In 1852, the *Detroit Free Press* claimed that the best joint for mutton was the saddle (the back loin), and it was always roasted. Another favorite were muttonchops broiled on a gridiron in the hearth. Finally, boiled mutton neck was served with mashed turnips and caper sauce.

Organ meats were commonly served and frequently combined with other foods. The following is a soup recipe from a Detroit cookbook published by the Detroit Friends of the Homeless and the Thompson Home for Old Ladies in 1873:

> *Take the head, pluck* [pluck is various organs, such as heart, kidney, liver or other] *and feet. Put them into a pot with cold water. Be careful to skim well when it boils. Chop a dozen small onions and let them all boil together until the meat cleaves from the bones…Cut all the meat from the head and feet, half the liver and lights* [lungs], *the whole of the heart and tongue; put all into the pot and boil about three-quarters of an hour. Before it is done take half a pound of butter with as much flour as will make into balls; stir until dissolved. Then add a pint of*

port wine, four hard boiled eggs cut in slices, and a lemon to improve the flavor. This will make two gallons, and may be kept several weeks, to be used as occasion requires.

Many other parts of animals were popular. Sweetbreads are the narrow thymus sweetbread in the throat and the smoother, rounder pituitary sweetbread in the stomach of a calf or lamb. Sweetbreads were loved by Detroiters. Over the years, there were many recipes for sweetbreads—nearly two hundred—published in the Detroit newspapers. Cookbook authors and columnists wrote menus and recipes for sweetbreads to be served at every meal of the day, usually boiled and then browned and crisped in hot oil.

Beef or lamb tongue was also a very common dish for late-night suppers, luncheons or brunches. Beef heart was frequently served, many times browned and then stuffed and baked. Tripe (stomach lining of beef) was another of the more common offal cuts. This recipe from the *Detroit Free Press* in 1884 uses curry powder:

Tripe Curry—boil two pounds of tripe cut into strips; peel two large onions and cut them into square pieces and put them into a stewpan with three tablespoons of butter. Let it stew until brown, stirring well and mixing in a tablespoon of curry powder. Now add one pint of milk and the cut up tripe. Let all stew for one hour…Serve in a deep dish with boiled rice.

"HEY, DOC, I GOT THIS PROBLEM…": A CURE FOR ANYTHING

The early cookbooks provided much more than recipes. They were also used as household management guides. They covered every conceivable issue or concern of a family: how to calculate interest on a bank loan, how to be a good conversationalist, how to raise canaries, how to develop good habits, tips for staying sober and being temperate, how to deal with unruly children, etc. Mrs. E. Hutchinson's book from 1854, *The Ladies Indispensable Companion*, tells women what color bonnet to wear:

Bestselling cookbook and remedy author Dr. Alvin Wood Chase and the title page from his famous cookbook.

STYLE OF BONNET

A person of delicate pale complexion should wear a hat with a pink lining.
A person of dark complexion should have white lining, with rose trimming.
A person with very red or yellow complexion should not wear high colors.

Many cookbooks included issues of health. Medicine did not exist or was ineffective; during the cholera epidemic in 1832, Detroit doctors prescribed drinking brandy. In general, health was maintained through proper diet and balance of food and modest living. However, most families lived in the dangerous world of the farm, where serious accidents were a common threat, and medical help was far away and not always useful. Most families at some time had an elderly parent to look after. It was the cookbook that provided answers on how to deal with these problems. Some cookbooks were actually sized to carry in aprons and accompanied families as they traveled in ox-driven covered wagons. Cookbook authors were regarded as essential advisors to families' well-beings. Many cookbook authors felt it was their duty to provide health advice to young families. Fannie Farmer suffered polio as a child and wrote extensively about nursing children, cooking for the sick and caring for invalids.

The Dreaded Michigan Itch and Ague

The settlers, from the 1820s through the 1850s, complained of ailments unique to Michigan. Ague was an intense malarial fever that produced cold and shakes followed by burning fever at regular intervals. V.P. Van Buren described the experience of ague in 1884:

> First the yawns and stretching stole upon you…they were soon followed by cold sensations, that crept over your system in streaks, faster and faster, and grew colder and colder…till the victim shook like an aspen leaf and his teeth chattered in his jaw…then commence the warm flashes until you reached the torrid region where you lay in burning heat, racked with pain in your head and along your back.

Shaking was so violent that settlers recalled plates falling off the log walls of the cabins.

The pioneers themselves explained the "fever and ague" as a consequence of the natural conditions of pioneering. According to their theory, the plowing of the land turned up decayed vegetation to the direct rays of the sun and "poisoned the air," and they noted that up to a certain point, "fever and ague" spread in proportion as settlement advanced. On the other hand, as the whole of a large area became cleared, the disease tended to disappear. The disease was more often annoying than fatal, attacking settlers in the season when they most needed to be well. It was observed to come on with the spring plowing and to last until the first frost in the fall, and there were few who were not troubled with "fever and ague" at some time during that period.

And everybody got it:

> Life was divided into well days and ague days. The minister made appointments to accommodate his "shakes." The constable watched the

well day of the witness to get him into court. Lawyer adjourned his case to avoid his ague day. The housewife regulated affairs by it.

It was treated with quinine, but since quinine was scarce, people developed their own unique remedies. Van Buren was told to "pare all my finger and toe nails, wrap the parings in tissue paper, then bore a hole in a maple tree, put in the nails and plug up the hole." This didn't work.

Settlers also commonly got something they called the Michigan itch. Here was one doctor's cure for Michigan itch, recorded by Alvin Wood Chase of Ann Arbor:

Take a pint bottle and put into it nitric acid 1 oz.; quicksilver 1 oz., and let stand until the silver is cut; then melt lard ½ lb. in an earthen bowl and mix all together, and stir with a wooden spatula until cold. Old Dr. Kittredge is an Allopathic Physician, but his ointment has been known, over the whole State, as death to the "Michigan or Prairie Itch," and the Doctor recommends it for Cancerous, Scrofulous, and Syphilitic Ulcers, also Salt-rheum, Ring-worms, "Pimpled Face," Chronic Inflammation of the eyelids, &c.

DOCTOR ALVIN WOOD CHASE

Alvin Wood Chase was born in New York in 1817, moved to Ohio and then settled in Marine City, Michigan, where he did various jobs. At the time, recipes for anything from food to treatments for sick animals were sold individually through mail order. They could be expensive—up to five dollars apiece. Chase saw an opportunity for a business collecting recipes and selling them as a book. To improve his credentials, he moved his family to Ann Arbor and enrolled at the University of Michigan Medical School. He did not complete a degree; he only audited classes since U of M required working knowledge of Latin, which Chase said he did not get in his "log school" in New York. He switched colleges, graduating with a medical degree in sixteen weeks from the Eclectic Institute of Cincinnati. He began buying medical or any practical recipes from country doctors, businessmen, farmers or grandmothers, taking pride that all ingredients were easily available to settlers, and some could be taken from the farmer's garden or the woods.

Dr. Chase's books were among the most popular publications of the nineteenth century, often claimed to be second in sales only to the Bible. The narration was anecdotal and chatty. It appealed to people of the day, and unlike other patent medicine salesmen, Chase was a medical doctor. He tested every recipe. The books went through dozens of editions, in at least two languages (English and German), and sold more than four million copies. Dr. Chase himself said his book had the largest sale of any book printed in America.

Chase was his own publisher and printer. His "Dr. Chase's Steam Printing House" building still stands at the corner of Miller and Main Streets in Ann Arbor. Never one for modesty, he described his print shop as "without question the finest printing office in the West." Chase was fifty-one when he celebrated the grand opening of his building in 1865 with four hundred in attendance. The next year, afraid that sales of his book would soon decline, and also convinced that he would die young, he sold the building and the rights to the books to Rice Beal of Ann Arbor. Sales did not decline. After Chase tried unsuccessfully to get back his book rights, he began an all-new recipe book. He died in 1885 (at age sixty-eight), just before completing the book, which was published posthumously as the "memorial edition."

His book *Dr. Chase's Recipes or Information for Everybody* offered eight hundred recipes for pea soup, pork chops, hair dye, boot polish and wood stain, followed by a cure for cancer or numerous other diseases. Here's a sample from the good Dr. Chase:

> *The Sex of Eggs—Mr. Genin lately addressed the Academy des Sciences, France, on the subject of the sex of eggs. He affirms that he is now able, after having studied the subject for upwards of three years, to state with assurance that the eggs containing the germ of males, have wrinkles on their smaller ends, while female eggs are smooth at the extremities.*

> *Counterfeit Money—Seven rules for detecting first examine the form and features of all human figures on the notes. If the forms are graceful and features distinct, examine the drapery—see if the folds lie natural; and the hair of the head should be observed, and see if the fine strands can be seen.*

> *Green Bay Indian's Remedy for Rheumatism—Wahoo, bark of the root, 1 oz.; blood root 1 oz.; black cohosh root 2 ozs.; swamp hellebore ½ oz.; prickly ash, bark or berries 1 oz.; poke root, cut fine, 1 oz.; rye whisky 1*

qt.; let stand a few days before using. DOSE—One tea-spoon every 3 or 4 hours increasing the dose to 2 or 3 tea-spoons, as the stomach will bear.

Soak the feet well and go to bed, covering up warm, and taking the "Sweating Drops" between each dose, as there directed, for three or four hours, and repeat the sweating every day until the disease surrenders to the treatment. If at any time the head feels too full, or the stomach sickens too much, drop down to the first dose of a tea-spoon, or even less, if necessary.

This prescription is from Jacob S. Cornelius, an Indian of Green Bay, who was very successful in Illinois, with it, in this disease.

Toad Ointment—For sprains, strains, lame-back, rheumatism, caked breasts. Good sized live toads, 4 in number; put into boiling water and cook very soft; then take them out and boil the water down to ½ pt., and add fresh churned, unsalted butter 1 lb. and simmer together; at the last add tincture of arnica 2 ozs. This was obtained from an old Physician, who thought more of it than of any other prescription in his possession. Some persons might think it hard on toads, but you could not kill them quicker in any other way.

A grateful customer sent Dr. Chase a thank-you letter:

Dr. A. W. Chase
Sir,
Before closing this, I think it is my duty to return you our hearty thanks for the benefit received from the Book. My wife was troubled with "enlarged neck"; she followed the directions of the Book; and I am happy to inform you it has made a perfect cure. I have tried a great many other of the "Recipes" with the same result. I would not be without the Book for fifty dollars.
Yours truly, James Ferguson

12

The Terror of Vegetables

Cholera in Detroit

We are obliged to announce to our readers that spasmodic cholera has made its appearance in this city. As might be expected, the prevalence of such a malignant disease among us has produced very general alarm among our citizens.
—Detroit Free Press, *July 12, 1832*

The year 1832 saw the first of several cholera epidemics rage across Detroit and the rest of the nation; a second, more virulent outbreak occurred in 1834, and additional outbreaks came in 1849 and 1854. In 1832, 7 percent of Detroit died of cholera. No one had any real idea what caused cholera at the time, but it was believed to be encouraged by intemperate living—any excessive behavior (especially drunkenness) could leave you open to the disease. *Any* excess. On July 19, 1832, the *Michigan Intelligencer* reported:

> *The second case is of a son of Hugh Bradford...His friends say that he drank too much cold water yesterday. He was taken in the night and died half past 11:00 this forenoon. His habits have become irregular.*

We now know that it is bacteria invading the digestive tract that causes severe diarrhea and vomiting, killing 50 percent of the people infected within hours through catastrophic loss of vital minerals and fluids. Detroiters did not know this in the summer of 1832; they only knew cholera was on its way.

The Honorable George C. Bates (1812–1886) was a practicing lawyer in Detroit when he arrived in 1833. He was a fine writer and one of the most celebrated campaign orators of his times. He wrote a column for the *Detroit Free Press* called "Bye Gone Days." President W.H. Harrison appointed him district attorney for Michigan. Sadly, he died in poverty.

Based on U.S. records that examined the history of the disease, cholera was "discovered" by English doctors in the Delta of the Ganges in India in 1817. It spread to Bombay in 1820 and then east to Africa and China; in 1821, it commenced its western march. It came up rivers and traveled roads and reached Russia and Moscow by 1830. By 1831, it had spread out across central Europe, and by October 1831, it reached Sunderland, England. In January 1832, it reached Edinburgh; in February, London; and in March, it was identified in Paris. In France, it was compared to a giant scythe slicing down people like stalks of wheat.

June 3, 1832, was declared the official date that cholera entered North America. While several Irish steamers from Dublin, Limerick and Cork had previously reached the Canadian quarantine station on the St. Lawrence Seaway suspected of carrying cholera, the steamer *Carrack* was recorded as the confirmed start. The following comes from *Carrack* quarantine records: "June 3rd. 145 emigrants from Dublin of whom 42 cholera deaths had occurred." In Robert Roberts's book *Sketches of the Straits*, published in 1884, he quotes a doctor of the day:

Cooking at Home

These emigrants were mostly poor Irishmen, packed away like sheep in the emigrant vessels with limited provisions and poor water to drink, and enduring a voyage from six to seven weeks. Was it any wonder that cholera should breed itself under such prolific circumstances?

The news reached Detroit, and a proclamation was published in the papers by the mayor on June 28, 1832:

Proclamation by Levi Cook, Mayor of the City of Detroit. Whereas, It appears the Asiatic Cholera now exists in the Province of Upper Canada and that it is expedient and desirable to use every precaution to prevent its introduction into this city...I do order and direct...no steamboat, schooner or other water craft, coming into the port of Detroit from any foreign port or place, shall approach any part of the city of Detroit nearer than one hundred yards.

On it came. Cholera quickly spread from Montreal and Quebec City to New York City. From New York, it was carried up rivers and roads to Buffalo, where U.S. troops under General Winfield Scott were stationed. Four ships were contracted by the United States to transport soldiers to Chicago to fight the Blackhawk War.

Cholera came to Detroit on one of those ships: the *Henry Clay*. (Ironically, Senator Henry Clay's son, a lieutenant, was on the ship and died of the disease.) The steamer *Henry Clay* was loaded with 370 U.S. soldiers headed to Chicago to fight the Blackhawk War. They set out from Buffalo on June 1. In Buffalo, cholera had been initially brought to the ship by a couple of soldiers, but by the time they reached the Detroit River on July 4, every solider on the ship showed symptoms of the disease. Immediately, the horrified Board of Public Health doctors realized the ship carried cholera, and it was ordered to dock at Belle Isle. But it was too late; the soldiers could not be controlled. They reached the dock at Fort Gratiot off Lake St. Clair. Half-crazed soldiers dove off the ship, fighting and mauling one another to get away from the horror of their diseased companions. Some were brought to an extemporized hospital. During the next several days, 150 soldiers ran to fields, died in the streets and fled to the woods, where they died alone. It was reported that wild animals devoured their dead bodies.

Two Detroiters who had communicated with the ship became infected; one died, and the other recovered. The next day, the Board of Health reported seventeen cases of infection, with nine dead.

After months of reports, news and rumors about the disease, near panic ensued in Detroit. The common council ordered giant potash pots to be placed on street corners, and pine resin and tar were burned, producing a thick black smoke to fumigate the air. In the damp, shady areas, they covered the ground with white powder, chloride of lime. They sent out a proclamation advising Detroiters on how to evade the disease. They printed articles that repeated the danger of drinking ardent spirits, poverty, excessive eating, unseemliness, extreme sunshine or cold at night, most types of food, wetness and cold drafts and ended with a dispiriting encouragement: "Above all be fearless and you will be safe."

One significant statement in the list was that the disease was not contagious; therefore, Detroit never set up quarantines and argued that they were counterproductive. That was a progressive view that conflicted with the conservative Whig belief that cholera was highly contagious and a punishment from God held by the cities outside Detroit, such as Pontiac, Rochester, Ann Arbor and Ypsilanti, settled primarily by evangelical New Englanders. Detroiters—mainly, if not mostly, French, some mixed breed (métis)—were seen as immoral sinners, and it was this divide that contributed to violence outside Detroit

At night, up and down the streets, the "death cart" walked, as if out of some medieval village ravaged by plague. The Detroit collector called out, "Bring out the dead! Bring out the dead!" He stopped ringing a bell for the dead as it tended to induce panic. As Zachariah Chandler remarked, "The living must have some sleep."

A large part of the fear people had of the disease, aside from the hideous, agonizing pain, stemmed from the swiftness with which it killed its victims. People went from happy and healthy to dead in less than twenty-four hours, many times in only a few hours. In her memoirs, Emily V. Mason, the older sister of Michigan's first governor, Stevens Mason, who lived in Detroit during the cholera period, wrote:

> *One evening a charming young man from Boston sat with us on the door-step, sipping a mint julep* [thought to be a preventive of the disease]. *He was well, gay, at parting; by the morning he was dead.*

George C. Bates was a writer and prominent Detroiter in the nineteenth century, and he wrote about his past experiences in the 1880s:

It is impossible now that fifty years have rolled away to describe the terror, alarm, and panic that prevailed, to depict or portray with the pen the blanched cheeks and husky voices of brave men who met at the corners of the streets or in the reception room and drinking room of the old Mansion House [brandy was prescribed by doctors as a way to prevent the disease]…[We] *could look up and down the avenue and see carts, drays and all kinds of vehicles on their way to the cemetery, filled with corpses, many of whom but a few hours before were in full health and strength.*

What Was Its Cause?

In 1849, the *Detroit Free Press* published the following article:

Cholera
Much has been written upon the subject of cholera…yet the disease preserves its former virulence; and the medical faculty proper as well as the itinerant Quack[s] *have not been able to arrest its progress or heal but few of its victims.*

Some believed that a continuous easterly wind for twenty-five days brought the pestilence from Europe. Wet clothes and chills were regularly discussed as a source. And although many medical experts recommended wholesome food, raw fruits and vegetables were considered dangerous. Nowadays, it is believed that it was the handling of the produce that passed along cholera; people did not wash their hands or the fruit. Many cookbooks of the time offered recipes for fresh fruits and vegetables, even salads, but not everyone trusted in their virtue. In 1832, the *New York Mirror* warned that fresh fruits should be forbidden to all classes, especially children. When cholera broke out in Detroit, fresh fruits immediately came under suspicion. During later epidemics in 1834 and 1849, the common council, on the advice of the Board of Health, passed an ordinance forbidding the sale of fresh fish, oysters, vegetables, fruits, veal and pork.

Another part of the panic in Detroit was due to the unpredictability of the spread of the disease; it did not move up streets in consistent progress but skipped past homes and jumped entire blocks. Detroit's population dropped from 5,000 to 1,500 as people fled the city. The grass grew high in the empty streets. George Bates wrote:

Despair was fast settling on all who remained. The stages were loaded down each succeeding morning with load after load of frightened people who fled in terror to Pontiac, to Jackson, and Monroe, and who not infrequently died on their way.

But the villages outside Detroit tore down bridges, erected blockades, threw up fences across roads and stationed armed guards, convinced Detroiters would bring cholera to their towns. A mail coach was stopped at gunpoint as it came to Ypsilanti, and the horses were shot and killed and the passengers ordered out. In Rochester, travelers were literally thrown out of hotels into the street, and armed gangs of men guarded the roads to Pontiac to prevent people from entering or sneaking in. Nevertheless, the disease spread, killing eleven in Marshall, Michigan.

The correspondent visiting Bloomfield Hills for the *Democratic Free Press* wrote at the end of July 1832: "Steady and temperate habits, and a disposition to submit to the will of God, are better safe guards against the cholera than the musket and bayonet, or the obstructing of highways."

Another commentary from the *Free Press* a week earlier read:

The consequences of this alarmed state may well be dreaded. It will lead to selfishness and cruel abandonment of those who may be taken ill, it will induce and inhumane and inhospitable treatment of strangers—it will induce conduct that will cause lasting regret—and above all it is one of the most active agents in multiplying cases of the dreaded disease.

Dr. Alvin Wood Chase from Ann Arbor wrote in frightening certainty:

Cholera morbus arises from a diseased condition of the bile, often brought on by over-indulgence with vegetables, especially unripe fruits; usually commencing with sickness and pain at the stomach, followed by the most excruciating pain and griping of the bowels, succeeded by vomiting and purging, which soon prostrate the patient. The person finds himself unavoidably drawn into a coil by the contraction of the muscles of the abdomen and extremities.

He recommended boiling green beans for two hours before serving them or what was left of them.

The press reported that someone passing a fruit stand laden with spoiled peaches had an attack of the "gripes"; therefore, "if bare proximity to those peaches caused him so much pain, the eating of them would have been certain death."

The association of cholera with fresh vegetables and other foods was made in 1832. All varieties of garden and market produce had been believed to transmit the deadly disease. The leading health scientists claimed that cholera had ravaged most fatally in the Delta of Ganges, where the Hindus lived largely on rice and vegetables; therefore, to escape the disease in the United States, one must restrict his diet to lean meat, potatoes, milk, tea and coffee.

In his cooking and medical advice books, Dr. Chase offered no fewer than nine cures for cholera. Here's one:

> Let me say that Merritt Blakeley, living near Flat Rock, Mich., came home from Detroit, during the last cholera season, having the cholera in its last stage, that is, with the vomiting, purging and spasms; the foregoing medicine being in the house, the wife, in her hurry and excitement, in place of two-thirds of a table-spoon, she read two-thirds of a tea-cup; and gave it accordingly, and saved his life…so, a mistake would be generally accredited for saving the patient, I say Providence did the work.

Among the city's most prominent doctors was Dr. Randal Rice, who was on the Board of Health in Detroit at that time the *Henry Clay* arrived at the docks of Detroit. George Bates reported that "under oath Dr. Rice declared that in 1832 he had saved nearly all his patients by bleeding and calomel, yet at this season [1834] every single patient who he had thus far treated had died upon his hands."

CURES FOR CHOLERA GREW MORE BIZARRE

In August 1832, the *Detroit Free Press* reported:

> A Mr. Wise is about introducing a system of ballooning…The patient is to ascend with the aid of a balloon to the height of about one mile. At this height the pressure of the atmosphere is so much diminished, that the blood rushes to the skin and relieves the disease…Wherever successful attempts have been made to bring the blood to the skin, the cure has been very generally effected.

The people and newspapers were so fed up with quack cures for cholera that they printed this "certain cure":

Take half a pint of hen's milk, 2 ounces of jeesway, and mix them in a hog's horn, stirring well with a cat's feather; then roll the mass of pills as big as a piece of chalk and long as a stick, and swallow them crosswise.

FEW DOCTORS AND NO HOSPITALS

Doctors were few in Detroit and soon became overwhelmed. There were no hospitals. As George Bates wrote in 1885, "To obtain nurses at night and aides and assistants to remove and bury the dead became almost impossible."

The doctors used volunteers to attend to the sick. When it was clear that a victim would not make it, the volunteer, with the doctor's approval, received permission to administer "Number 6"—arsenic.

In 1832, Father Gabriel Richard visited each of his church families' homes without cease, encouraging the healthy and administering last rights to the dying. It was said he worked himself to exhaustion and showed signs of cholera. He succumbed to the disease in September 1832. Despite the dreadful fear of the disease, his funeral was attended by thousands of people, many more than the population of Detroit at that time.

In 1833, a Swiss priest in his twenties arrived in Detroit to begin an orphanage for the poor. He was an outstanding individual, educated in Rome, strong and dedicated, who a few years earlier had served on the Papal Swiss Guards for the pope. His size made him a good fit for the Swiss Guards—he was six feet tall and over two hundred pounds; in his day, he was imposing. His name was Father Martin Kundig. He could be a cheerful, fun man who sang and played guitar for the children and organized theatrical productions, including Shakespeare.

Soon after he arrived, cholera broke out again in Detroit, this time more virulent than in 1832. He immediately had workmen arrange an old church on Bates Street into a hospital, with one side for women and the other for men. He took a horse and cart to pick up victims and return to the hospital, where he would carry them on his back to a cot. Often, on the very the same day, he carried them on his back again, out of the hospital and into

Father Gabriel Richard.

Father Martin Kundig.

the cart to be buried. His good work was described in the *Michigan State Senate* in 1838:

> *He brought in every person without respect to sect or denomination, Jew or Gentile, Presbyterian or Methodist, of every color, if they belonged to the human family, he took them in and provided for them.*

In her autobiography much later, Emily Mason, sister of Governor Mason, commented on Father Kundig:

> *When the cholera appeared in Detroit, this good priest distinguished himself in another field; he was at every bed-side, in every house, carrying in his arms the sick and dying to his improvised hospital.*

He was so close to the disease—he was described later as "calm…walking through this valley of death"—that people began to shun him, afraid he might be contaminated. He became overwhelmed as cholera victims were dumped from boats onto docks or thrown out of buildings to die in the streets and alleys. He turned to his church's youth for help. He was so compelling and absolute in his conviction to help victims and in his fearless example that he convinced about twenty-five "sweet young girls," as the *Free Press* called them, such as Anne Dequindre (age fifteen), Emile and Angelique Campau (daughters of Barnabe Campau, who owned a commercial fishing operation on Belle Isle), the Morans, the Beaubiens, the Knagg sisters and Josephine Desnoyer, to help him in the church hospital. The girls and young women would take the cart to pick up infected wretches, the poor, children, filthy drunks, dead bodies—any and all lying on the streets, lanes, steamers and docks in the extremely dangerous conditions—to perform, as the newspaper described, "irksome and sickening duties" and cart them back to the church to save them through nursing or to gently prepare them for a dignified grave. Their courage became well known throughout the city and inspired other Detroiters to "be fearless" and not succumb to dread. The popular social historian of Detroit Friend Palmer remembered the girls and wrote about the epidemic:

> *Let it be borne in mind and never be forgotten that of that noble, old Catholic priest and all those bright, beautiful, beaming, blessed Catholic girls, not one of them although exposed day by day, night by night for weeks together during the existence of that dreadful epidemic ever were even attacked by that hideous monster, the cholera.*

Once the disease departed, it left orphans, many from good families who had never known poverty. Father Kundig was placed in charge as superintendent of the orphanage poorhouse. The expenses were high, and he took payment from the county in the form of county warrants, which in the economic collapse of 1837 proved worthless. He incurred much debt, caring for eighty to one hundred orphans; he still owed a coffin maker $500 for coffins. He claimed later that he was much humiliated by the debts and eventually the creditors had had enough. They took everything. They took his horses, stoves, carpets and books, his little guitar and even the clothing off the children. Kundig sat beside naked children, some staring at him with nowhere to go but the street. The women of St. Anne's managed an emergency charity and brought him some money, blankets and more clothes for the children. Kundig found them a log cabin outside the city where they could shelter and then sadly dispensed them to farmers, where they were compelled to work until families could be found for them.

Kundig remained a few years more in Detroit. In 1841, he was elected a regent of the University of Michigan. He was honored by the State of Michigan, and $3,000 was appropriated to reimburse him for—and to continue—his work through great effort by Governor Stevens Mason, but it didn't come close to covering his debts. The church soon transferred him to Milwaukee, where he helped immigrating German Catholics and eventually was made victor general of Milwaukee. But it took him decades to pay back the debt incurred in Detroit. In 1865, years later, living in Milwaukee, he wrote an open letter published in the *Detroit Free Press*:

> *Now, after being sixty years old, I have my long desire fulfilled, viz: Not to die before I had satisfied my creditors. I have now the great satisfaction to state that I have paid my debts—God be praised for it! All excepting two creditors, whom I do not know where to find.*

Father Kundig died in 1879, "full of years, full of honors, and full of holiness."

13

Wild Game on the Table

Wild game was among the most popular items sold to Detroiters and exported across the country. Since the eastern United States was hunted out by this time, Detroit and other cities in the West became major suppliers of wild game that was shipped via the Erie Canal. Typically, venison, boar or wild birds were served as a separate course at dinner parties or on holidays. In addition, many Detroiters or country people in the early 1800s ate mostly game, so there was a strong demand for it. The following advertisement ran in the *Detroit Free Press* in 1859:

> *To the Lovers of Good Things!*
> *Gentlemen! Do you see that large sign New York House of Refreshments, a few doors down from the corner of Jefferson Avenue at Griswold St. This is to give notice that Patrick Collins, proprietor, is about to open his Fall arrival consisting of every variety of Wild Game, Pheasants, Ducks, Snipe, Woodcock, Teal, &c. which when served up by his celebrated cook will make an epicure's mouth water. He shortly expects to have Oysters in the shell and an importation of Sea Green Turtle.*

The availability of game seemed to prove that Americans in the 1800s would literally eat anything. Wild game was especially popular at Thanksgiving, made clear from an article in the *Free Press* from 1882:

THE LUXURIES YOU CAN HAVE FOR DINNER AND WHAT THEY WILL COST
"Are we going to have much of a Thanksgiving this year?" inquired a Free
Press *reporter of a game and fruit dealer at the market yesterday; who in
thirty years has not been absent from his stand in as many days.*
"Yes, Sir, as big a one as ever known..."
"How about prices? Can poor people afford a big dinner?"
"Certainly they can. Prices are generally quite low."

The reporter stopped by the store of H.T. Phillips, which was located on
Michigan Avenue. Phillips was the leading purveyor of wild game in the city
and claimed to be the biggest supplier of venison in the United States for
several decades starting in 1862:

> *Bob Baker of H.T. Phillips and Co. was found contemplating a big black
> bear that had just been left by a truck in front of the store while further back
> on the sidewalk lay three others.*
> *"Hello, Bob! What are you going to do with your bears?"*
> *"I wish I had more of them. That fellow over there goes to the Russell
> House, that one to the Brunswick, and that one to the Griswold. This one
> has just come in and isn't sold yet. He'd make a fine roaster for some private
> family, wouldn't he?"*
> *"How much does he weigh?"*
> *"Three hundred and fifty."*
> *"How much per pound?"*
> *"Twenty cents."*
> *"Send him up!"*

Along with bear, recipes can be found for squirrel pie, porcupine, possum
and rabbit. Birds were especially popular, with hundreds of thousands of
birds migrating up the Detroit River. Generally, wild game recipes differed
little from our own, although an unusual recipe for duck, printed in the
Detroit Free Press in 1865, is as follows:

> *The intestines of the bird should be taken out by a small hole at the vent,
> and the inside washed out and stuffed...with bread crumbs or crackers and
> chopped meat, then wet the feathers thoroughly and cover with hot embers.
> When the cooking is finished, peel off the burnt feathers and skin and you
> will find beneath a lump of nice white flesh, which, when once taste will
> never be forgotten.*

Butchering a turtle to make turtle soup.

Terrapin or green turtles were popular throughout the eighteenth and nineteenth centuries when turtles could still be found in the wild. In the 1700s on the East Coast, where turtles could be gathered by the "shovelful," New York City turtle barbecues were all the rage, and in Detroit, turtle was just as popular. Recipes for turtle steaks were found in the *Detroit Free Press* in 1847. Like oysters, terrapin was frequently sold "all you can eat" at Detroit saloons or inns. It was a featured soup at banquets and weddings. In the 1850s, a saloon at the corner of Griswold and Larned Streets offered "Terrapin Lunch." The terrapins were brought from New York by the saloon owner, Alfred Thomas, who turned them into soup. Here is his advertisement in the *Detroit Free Press* in 1852:

> GREEN TURTLE
> One of these "shell fish," just two days from the briny deep will be served up today at Peverelly's. Families and others will be provided with turtle soup at all hours.

A few daring souls would try to make turtle soup at home. If someone had a taste for turtle soup—real turtle soup—it was time to roll up the sleeves. The following is a recipe for turtle soup from Mrs. Chadwick, a well-known cookbook author of the day:

> *For one fifty to sixty pound turtle…*
> *Tie it up by the hind fin, the head being downward, tie the fore fins or it will be troublesome to manage. Take the head in your left hand and cut off the neck as near the head as possible. Have one or two tubs of water ready and when you cut up the turtle lay it on its back, when you must run the knife between the caliapee and caliapash…always keep the edge of your knife on the side of the breast, else you may break the gall and then it would be entirely spoiled.*

Another cookbook, *The Women's' Suffragette Cookbook* from 1886, offered:

> *Decidedly the terrapin has to be killed before cooking, and the killing is often no easy matter. The head must be cut off, and, as the [terrapin's] sight is peculiarly acute, the cook must exercise great ingenuity in concealing the deadly weapon. I have known half an hour to be consumed in the effort.*

It must have been an interesting sight to watch a housewife lugging home a live sixty-pound turtle from the market.

FROGGIN'

Because of the once-vast St. Clair flats and marshland down by Monroe, bullfrogs were everywhere. And they were enormous, commonly seven pounds. A frog that weighed nine pounds was on display at the central market. When one considers that the average whole chicken at the supermarket today weighs about five pounds, these were very big frogs. Their legs were described to be "as long as drumsticks." Detroit was known throughout the country as the frog leg capital.

Frogs were not worth catching until they reached two years of age and were not in their prime until age five. They were hard to catch, being very shy and quick to escape. Frog hunters caught them from the shore but also out of small flat-bottomed boats that they would pole silently through the marsh on hot summer days. The hunters used a strong fishing line with a large hook, which they manipulated to snag the frog. Some had long poles and fishing line that they would lower near the frog; the end had hooks and a small piece of red flannel, which they claimed the bullfrog "charged." Forked frogging spears were occasionally used. Many carried small "cat and rat" shotguns, shooting the frogs with mustard seed. Good hunters caught two hundred frogs a day, but most caught a few dozen.

Fred Butcher from Fenton, Michigan, started a frog ranch on his farm. He had the bullfrogs penned in a farm pond and, by 1907, shipped 17,350 dozen frog legs across the country. He was one of the largest frog legs farmers in the United States. He had a staff of men who spent their days catching bullfrogs all summer. On summer nights, the croaking bullfrogs could be heard for miles.

Only the legs of the frog are eaten. They were skinned first, soaked several times in cold water, salted and then dipped in batter or breadcrumbs and cooked in hot oil. President Grover Cleveland's favorite dish was Detroit frog legs rolled in cracker crumbs and then pan fried in butter.

Frenchtown and Their Muskrat

Detroit began as a French village, and those earliest French families occupied both sides of the Detroit River. Their farms stretched from Port Huron down to Lake Erie and northern Ohio. However, by the early decades of the 1800s, more Americans (especially New Englanders) began arriving, causing some misunderstandings and, in some cases, mutual dislike.

One New England tourist, Cyrus P. Bradley, was sixteen when he wrote the following journal of his time in Detroit in 1834:

> We arrived at Detroit about half past two and I spent the afternoon in walking around the city…On the little narrow street, near the river…is settled by the French, the descendants of the original proprietors. They are a singular people—hate the Yankees—will not mix with them, will not suffer their children to learn the language or have any intercourse with them.

More and more New Yorkers and New Englanders poured into Detroit by the thousands. The French began migrating away from Detroit to St. Clair Shores and farther downriver, purchasing land from local native tribes, such as the Wyandots.

The native tribes showed the French inhabitants the bounty of wildlife that lived in the rivers and the marshy shores along the rivers and Lake Erie; this included frogs, millions of ducks and geese, turtles, wild rice and the now-famous muskrat. A local historian and expert on regional French culture in Monroe County, Ralph Naveaux, has written about the archaeological remains of the Native Americans that show the native populations in the region had been eating muskrats long before the arrival of the French. The French residents ate so many muskrats that they became known as *Mushrat* (pronounced Moosh-rat) French.

The Catholic Church and Muskrats

The debate continues today about whether the Catholic Church allowed people in the region to substitute muskrat for fish on Ash Wednesday and on Fridays in Lent. The story goes that after the Battle of the River Raisin in the War of 1812, local families escaped with nothing but their lives and were starving and freezing to death in the middle of Lent. They asked Father Gabriel Richard if they might substitute the muskrat for traditional fish to survive; after all, it lives in water like the fish, they reasoned. It is claimed that he allowed them to do this. However, this is disputed. There is nothing in writing from the church on this issue, and some in the church deny that this was ever a "dispensation." There is also argument about whether this was applied to all of the French living in the region or to only the Reau family in Maumee Bay near Toledo, now called Erie Township.

This question will likely never be answered; however, muskrat has become a part of *la cuisine regionale*, and whether it was substituted for fish no longer matters much. Before the invasion of McDonalds and the like, this local cuisine became well known in Detroit. Ralph Naveaux writes that at the start of the twentieth century, many small guesthouses could be found along the water. For fifty cents, a patron could select a live fish from a weir (holding net) at the dock, to be followed by platters of fried chicken, mashed potatoes and frog legs. The muskrat dinners and fundraisers held during Lent had spread beyond the French to include Germans in Monroe and Polish residents in downriver Detroit.

Muskrat has a long heritage in the cuisine of Monroe. In November 1815, two boys were traveling with their uncle on a small boat from Buffalo to Harsens Island in Lake St. Clair to meet up with their father, who had bought property on the island to start a farm. Near Put-in-Bay on Lake Erie, their boat went aground and broke apart. The boys and the other four men had nothing dry to wear and no food. Some hunters appeared on the marsh with a small bag of flour, a lidded Dutch oven and a dozen dressed muskrats. One of the men, a sailor named Jack, began to cook up the catch, as described by A. Stewart, one of the boys, sixty years later (1879) for the *Detroit Free Press*:

> [Jack] *proceeded to cook them in the only way possible at the time. He put part of the flour in a tin pan, poured water into it, then stirred with a stick until it became a stiff dough, made flat by the pressure of the hands; the muskrats [were] quartered and all was placed in the iron [pot] and placed over a brisk fire. After the contents were thought ready to serve they were placed in portions on the foresail [front of the boat] and brother and I were told to use a little paddle which had been whittled out for us...I have eaten often of grandmothers' puddings and pumpkin pies, none of which were relished better.*

One does not just cook muskrat; there are well-defined rules for preparation. Dennis Au, a former resident and descendant of French Canadian residents of Monroe, described the preparation:

> *The rodent must be trapped in Winter. It is imperative to remove all fat and musk glands before the animal is parboiled with onions, celery and spices. When tender the rat is either fried with onions or roasted with creamed corn. This twice-cooked process is essential.*

The 1905 muskrat-hunting season began in November and continued until April. Professional muskrat hunters, such as Monsieur Charles Laforet, considered one of the best muskrat hunters on the River Rouge, did not shoot muskrat but trapped them. The furs were usually in demand, and muskrat meat was becoming popular in Detroit. They were featured on the menus of the Black Cat Club and the Game Cock Club. "If I could

Hunting muskrats.

kill two hundred a day I'd sell them all," Monsieur Laforet claimed in a 1905 interview.

But hunting with rifles was popular with sportsmen. The marsh grass was burned off to prevent wounded animals from escaping. Amateur hunters were sometimes helped by hunting guides. The little beasts were hard to hit. In 1905, an amateur hunter named Judge Phelan was taken out in a marsh boat to shoot muskrat in East Sandwich (Windsor, Ontario) by the guide Wolfgang Feilers, commonly known as "Wolf." Wolf stood with the judge while he took some target shots to loosen up. The judge was well equipped and was described as looking like Buffalo Bill Cody without the goatee. The judge and the guide climbed in the boat and soon saw a muskrat on the weeds.

The judge pulled up his flintlock rifle, "Shall I shoot now?"

"No," said Wolf. "Let me row closer."

The judge prepared to sneak up on the rat. Nearer and nearer they drew.

"Shall I shoot now?" he whispered.

"Judge, now prepare to shoot."

The judge prepared.

"Now, Judge, un-cock your gun."

The boat drifted silently closer.

The judge released the hammers of his weapon.

"Now, Judge! Hit him over the head with the gun!"

Which he did and bagged his muskrat. Wolf explained that he had watched the judge practice his shooting earlier and determined that the clubbing method was his best bet.

WHOOPING IT UP WITH THE MUSKRAT

In 1904, the Monroe Yacht Club decided to host a big affair that it dubbed the "Muskrat Carnival." Yacht club funds were low due to the debt of the new clubhouse. They hoped the Muskrat Carnival held on December 28 would bring them back to prosperity. In charge was Commodore W.C. Sterling.

Invitations went to neighboring yacht clubs such as Toledo, Detroit and others. Old Boys Clubs of the region were also invited. Electric interurban rails would haul revelers into Monroe and back from Toledo to Detroit throughout the night. The yacht club secured two hundred muskrats to cook up and a makeshift gambling casino. It was so popular that in the next years, it cooked up five to six thousand muskrats and had attendees from across the country.

The *Detroit Free Press* reported in 1905 "about 3,000 men and three women being in attendance." Red, white and blue bunting decorated the Monroe Armory with a huge "Welcome" banner to greet the ratters. Alongside the armory, a makeshift bar was set up, and Detroit bartenders served drinks as fast as they could and kept things jolly. In 1905, the mayor of Chicago was supposed to attend. Yacht teams from as far away as New York and Seattle showed up. A German band came down from Detroit. They were late because the electric interurban car they road collided with a beer wagon in Wyandotte. They made "quite a stir" when they came through the doors. The German band members were convinced to dress in French colors and play French songs but declined to eat French food and "de mooshrats."

As the famous columnist and writer from Detroit Edgar Guest observed:

> *Those who are partial to rat as food, attacked the rat first, leaving the coleslaw, celery and potatoes, etc. until the last. With the man who is eating rat for the first time things are reversed. He shows a remarkable fondness for coleslaw and tries to put away as much celery as possible.*

At midnight, it was still going strong. Roars of laughter filled the hall following the "oriental dance" of a "Madam" LaBeau, who at the conclusion of the performance threw off her wig and showed (s)he was one of the boys. The last to leave was a Detroit newspaperman, who was found wandering in Monroe with a large box of cooked muskrats under his arm "for the boys in the office." The mayor of Toledo, Sam Jones, got home early the next morning to find that someone had stuck a live muskrat in his coat pocket.

Conclusion

There is wonderful advice by bestselling author and authority on food and nutrition Michael Pollan that goes: "Don't eat anything your great-grandmother wouldn't recognize as food." This is a warning against manufactured products with unrecognizable ingredients posing as real, simple food. Looking back on Detroit's past, I would suggest a counter argument to Mr. Pollan's words: "Your great-grandmother ate a lot of stuff you would not recognize as food."

In my view, people feel an urgency to know about their past, perhaps because if we don't know about our past, in some ways we don't know who we are today. So this book is not about remembering who Detroiters were but about seeing who they were for the first time. Instead of the big issues, I prefer the everyday stuff: the history of insignificant things. Many people, when handed lengthy books or reports, say, "Skip the details, get to the point." I can't do that. It is the daily stuff that connects us to people just like us from the past. The details are all that interest me. There is no "point"; it's just living. I don't care what year the Erie Canal was built. I want to know what kind of sandwiches the people ate on the boats. I want to hunt gigantic bullfrogs with my "cat and rat" gun. Or ride a camel through downtown at the Shriner convention. In my life, I can safely say I have never seen anyone butcher a turtle. I want to feel the roar of 100 million pigeons flying overhead. I've never tricked a neighbor into putting his nose in hot chicken gravy. But I would like to.

Bibliography

Beecher, Catharine Esther, and Harriett Beecher Stowe. *The American Woman's Home*. New York: J.B. Ford And Company, 1869.

Blot, Pierre. *Handbook of Practical Cookery for Ladies and Professional Cooks. Containing the Whole Science and Art of Preparing Human Food. By Pierre Blot. Professor of Gastronomy, and Founder of the New York Cooking Academy*. New York: D. Appleton and Co., 1868.

Blouin, Francis. "Not Just Automobiles: Contributions of Michigan to the National Economy, 1866–1917." In *Michigan: Visions of Our Past*. Edited by Richard J. Hathaway. East Lansing: Michigan State University Press, 1989.

Blum, Peter H. *Brewed In Detroit: Breweries and Beers Since 1830*. Detroit, MI: Wayne State University Press, 1999.

Bohn-Bettoni Collection. Including two thousand restaurant menus, 1870–1930. UNLV.

Bolles, Albert S. *Industrial History of the United States*. Norwich, CT: H. Bill Publishing Co., 1879.

Burton, Clarence. *The City of Detroit Michigan, 1701–1922*. Vol. 3. Detroit, MI: S.J. Clark Company, 1922.

Catlin, George, and Robert B. Ross. *Landmarks of Detroit: A History of the City, revised by Clarence W. Burton*. Detroit, MI: Evening News Association, 1898.

Cummings, Richard Osborn. *The American and His Food*. Chicago: University of Chicago Press, 1940.

DeVoe, Thomas Farrington. *The Market Assisstant*. New York: Hurd and Houghton, 1867.

Ericson, Wilma Wood, ed. *The Gilded Age Comes to Detroit, Detroit Perspectives*. Detroit, MI: Wayne State University Press, 1991.

Farmer, Silas. *History of Detroit and Michigan or Metropolis Illustrated Past and Present*. Detroit, MI: self-published, 1889.

Freidman, Watler A. *Birth of a Salesman*. Cambridge, MA: Harvard University Press, 2004.

Hale, Sarah Josepha Buell. *The Good Housekeeper*. Boston: Weeks, Jordon and Company, 1839.

Hamlin, Marie Caroline Watson. *Legends of Le Detroit*. Detroit, MI: Thorndike Nourse, 1884.

Harris, Howell J. "Conquering Winter: U.S. Consumers and the Cast-Iron Stove." *Building Research and Information* 36, no. 4 (July 2008): 337–50

———. "Inventing the U.S. Stove Industry, c. 1815–1875: Making and Selling the First Universal Consumer Durable." *Business History Review* 82, no. 4 (Winter 2008): 701–33.

———. "The Stove Trade Needs Change Continually: Designing the First Mass-Market Consumer Durable, c. 1830–1900." *Winterhur Portfolio* (Winter 2009).

Henderson, Mary. *Practical Cooking and Dinner Giving*. New York: Harper and Brothers, 1877.

Howland, Ester Allen. *The New England Economical Housekeeper, and Family Receipt Book*. Cincinnati, OH: H.W. Derby, 1845.

Johnson, Peter Leo, DD. *Stuffed Saddlebags: The Life of Martin Kundig, Priest, 1805–1879*. Milwaukee, WI: Bruce Publishing Company, 1942.

Langone, Jan. Commentary and Biographical Notes on Maria Parloa. "Feeding America" archive of cookery books, Michigan State University, 2004. ["Feeding America" is funded by the Institute of Museum and Libraries Services, an independent federal agency that supports the nation's museums and libraries. Ms. Jan Langone is curator of American culinary history, Clements Library, University of Michigan.]

Leake, Paul. *History of Detroit*. Vols. 2 & 3. Chicago: Lewis Publishing Company, 1912.

Leslie, Eliza. *Directions for Cooker: In Its Various Branches, by Miss Leslie*. Philadelphia: E.L. Carey and Hart, 1840.

Lincoln Dinner Menu. Lincoln House, U.S. National Park Service brochure.

March, Walter (Olando). *Shoe Pac Recollections: A Wayside Glimpse of American Life*. New York: Bunce and Brother, 1856.

Mershon, W.B. *The Passenger Pigeon*. New York: Outing Publishing Company, 1907.

Mitchell, Paul. *Detroit in History and Commerce*. Detroit, MI: Rogers and Thorpe Publishers, 1891.

Parloa, Maria. *Miss Parloa's New Cookbook and Guide to Marketing*. Boston: Estes and Lauret, 1880.

————. *Young Housekeeper*. Boston: Estes and Lauriat, 1894.

Porterfield, James D. *Dining by Rail: The History and the Recipes of America's Golden Age of Railroad Cuisine*. New York: St. Martin's Press, 1993.

Roberts, Robert E. *Sketches of the City of the Straits*. Detroit, MI: Detroit Free Press and Job Printing, 1884.

Roethke, Theodore. *The Collected Poems of Theodore Roethke*. New York: Doubleday, 1961.

Root, Waverly, and Richard De Rochement. *Eating in America: A History*. New York: Echo Press, 1976.

Rorer, Sarah Tyson. *Mrs. Rorer's New Cookbook*. Philadelphia: Arnold and Company, 1902.

Sanderson, J.M. *The Complete Cook Plain and Practical Directions for Cooking and House Keeping*. Philadelphia: J.B. Lippincott Co., 1864.

Schneider, John C. *Detroit and the Problem of Order, 1830–1880: A Geography of Crime, Riot, and Policing*. Lincoln: University of Nebraska Press, 1980.

Schwartz, James Z. *Conflict on the Michigan Frontier: Yankee and Borderland Cultures, 1815–1840*. DeKalb: Northern Illinois University Press, 2009.

Severence, Henry Ormal. *Michigan Trailmakers*. Ann Arbor, MI: George Wahr Publisher, 1930.

Stasser, Susan. *Never Done. A History of American Housework*. N.p.: Owl Books, 2000.

Tanty, Francois. *La Cuisine Française French Cooking for Every Home. Adapted to American Requirements*. Chicago: Baldwin, Ross & Co. Publishers, Masonic Temple, 1893.

Wallace, Mary J. *Historic Photos of Detroit*. Nashville, TN: Turner Publishing Company, 2007.

Woodford, Frank B., and Arthur M. Woodford. *All Our Yesterdays: A Brief History of Detroit*. Detroit, MI: Wayne State University Press, 1969.

About the Author

Bill Loomis is a freelance writer living in Ann Arbor, Michigan. Mr. Loomis has a degree in comparative literature from the University of Michigan and has done graduate work in television production at New York University. He has had articles published in the *New York Times*, *Quality Magazine*, a variety of business academic journals, *Michigan History Magazine* and the *Detroit News* online.

Visit us at
www.historypress.net

www.ingramcontent.com/pod-product-compliance
Lightning Source LLC
Chambersburg PA
CBHW070838100426
42813CB00003B/667